*Bob, My Dad the Fisherman:
A Father and Son's Relationship*

Bob, My Dad the Fisherman:
A Father and Son's Relationship

By

Raymond Greenlaw

Roxy Publishing, LLC
Savannah, Georgia
United States of America

Copy Editor—Hugh Willoughby
Cover Design—Robert Greenlaw
Photographer—Rox-Ellene Greenlaw
Additional Design—Wongduean Bohthong
Text Design—Raymond Greenlaw
Typesetting—WORD – Garamond 12

Roxy Publishing, LLC
Apache Avenue, Box 411
Savannah, Georgia 31419 USA

http://drraymondgreenlaw.com

Second edition, paperback.

© By Raymond Greenlaw, 2018
All rights reserved.

No portion of this work may be reproduced, stored in a retrieval system, or transmitted in any form or by any means—electronic, mechanical, photocopying, recording, or otherwise—without prior written permission of the publisher.

The trade names and trademarks of several companies and products have been used in this book. No endorsement of them nor any association with this book should be inferred.

ISBN 978-1-947467-05-7 (paper)

Dedication

For my dear mother, Rox-Ellene Greenlaw, with love.

For my dear father, Robert Greenlaw, I miss you!

Table of Contents

Dedication v

Preface vii

Chapter 1 Angry Geese 1

Chapter 2 Largemouth Bass 13

Chapter 3 World-Record Eel 27

Chapter 4 Hooked Fisherman 37

Chapter 5 Beautiful Rainbow Trout 51

Figures 63

Chapter 6 Trout Fisherman Captured 95

Chapter 7 Calendar Pickerel 103

Chapter 8 Alaskan Halibut 117

Epilogue 129

About the Author 137

Other Books by Raymond Greenlaw 138

Preface

This book is about my father, his love of fishing, our relationship, and my memories about him. Since these stories are about fishing, they really need no further explanation or justification. I've taken some poetic license here and there, but more or less stuck to the facts. My Dad was indeed a world record holder. You'll learn more about my father, and my relationship with him, as you read. My Dad was born during the Great Depression. That event shaped his life and his thinking. It placed limits on him that he wasn't able to overcome. He wasn't perfect, and he knew it. My Dad was a smart man and raised me the best that he could. He provided me with as much love as he could. His love came in the form of companionship.

Men who were raised during the Great Depression needed to be tough for they'd endured tough times. They weren't huggers; they felt that they needed to display great strength. I accepted my Dad for who he was. He was a sensitive man, who when confronted with his shortcomings, admitted them and tried to improve himself. Throughout his years, he grew and became a better person. I am extremely lucky that my father spent so much time with me. Although my father was an extremely busy man, he always gave freely of his time for me. Many fathers in modern times aren't available for their children. Children are left to occupy their time using electronics such as mobile phones and tablets. My father demonstrated things to me in a hands-on manner, shared his hobbies with me, and was an active teacher. He didn't send me out to play on my own or buy me an expensive electronic device to babysit me. I'm exceptionally grateful for what we were able to share.

Fishing was perhaps my father's greatest love after my mother, Roxy. He read widely about fishing and researched the latest techniques. He watched television shows about fishing and discussed recent innovations down at the bait shop. While picking the brains of other local fishermen, he'd make metal notes where the deep holes were, what lures the fish were hitting, and the best time of day to seek out "The Big One." My Dad practiced state-of-the-art methods. He utilized the best practices and latest technologies. If he thought something could improve his success, he employed it. He spoke widely with others who shared his passion. My father was not among the best fishermen I ever met; he *is* the best fisherman I ever met.

I hope that you'll enjoy *Bob, My Dad the Fisherman*. In this second edition I've expanded the book. I've also created an electronic version of it. It's been almost twenty years now since my Dad stopped fishing. I still feel an emptiness inside, and I miss sharing our lives together. I miss his guidance, friendship, and love. Our bond seems to grow stronger as the years past. As I grow older and gain more perspective on life, I can understand more clearly why my Dad lived his life the way that he did. As you read this book, you can see the types of relationships that fathers and sons used to have. Relationships where they shared vast amounts of time together, where they made time for each other, where they challenged each other to become better people, and where they strengthened their relationship through mutual respect, acceptance, and understanding. I won't ever get to see my father again and that hurts, but at least I can share our relationship with you, dear reader. And, when I miss my Dad, I can turn to these pages. Here I can hear his voice, see him smile, and talk to him. He becomes alive again, and I can feel his passion.

I hope you're resting comfortably, Dad. Your loving son, Raymond.

Raymond Greenlaw
April 7, 2018
Reprinted: December 2, 2021

Bob, My Dad the Fisherman:
A Father and Son's Relationship

Chapter 1
Angry Geese

My father's name is Robert Wilson Greenlaw, but nearly everyone knew him as Bob. I never called him Bob, but simply Dad. Dad fished whenever he had the chance. He made time for fishing, as that was his passion. My Dad was a very organized and efficient person, and he seemed to have more free time than most fathers. It was a good thing that he grew up near water in the city of Worcester, Massachusetts, because the thing that he loved the most in life, besides his wife (my mother Roxy), was fishing. I can say that few people ever develop a passion for anything in life as strongly as my Dad's passion for fishing. He was obsessed, and he knew it.

I never talked to my father about his love of fishing; I simply knew that he loved fishing, both fresh and saltwater, and always had. His love of fishing ran deep, very deep. If Bob had grown up in any other location in the world anywhere near water, I am certain that he would've been a fisherman. Had he grown up in a desert—well, I don't really know what his life would've been like. I am pretty darn sure that he would've found his way to water though. His calling seemed to be fishing. That is what made him happy. He could lose himself on the water to life's daily issues. But, he never lost his concentration on fishing.

My Dad's passion for fishing was great. Like Chuck Yeager's desire to fly, Richard Feynman's desire to advance science, or Mother Teresa's desire to help the poor, my father loved to fish. He didn't fish to drink beer. He didn't fish to kill time. He didn't fish to be one of the guys. My father simply loved fishing. He fished because that is what he loved and wanted to do. Fishing came natural to him.

Dad developed a Zen-like approach to fishing, and rarely left anything to chance. His systematic way of preparing for a fishing trip was crafted through years and years of experience, and in his seventy years of fishing, he'd probably fished close to seven-thousand times. While I would be concentrating on organizing my fishing-pole and tackle-box, my Dad would effortlessly and without thought be able to assemble everything else for a trip. He always brought along a handful of old towels to tidy up after a catch. My Dad was a neatnik, and now so am I.

My Mom would often pack us a lunch which would go into one of the numerous coolers that we'd stored in the kitchen of our home. I would get three sandwiches and some cookies, whereas my Dad would usually have just one sandwich. He weighed only 138 pounds and was wiry and fit. The contents of the cooler were kept cool by plastic-bottles filled with ice. When the ice melted, we drank the cold water. Once the car was loaded and the canoe affixed to its roof, we would say goodbye to my mother, and off we would go, hearing her say "Good luck" whenever we departed.

Although Rhode Island is a small state, it's home to many bodies of water. Many of these beautiful ponds were carved out during the most-recent ice age. My Dad and Mom fished in nearly all of Rhode Island's ponds, including a handful of private ones. My father would often talk to land owners and attempt to get their permission to fish in their private ponds. Since few fishermen, if any, fished in such waters, the fishing there was usually exceptional. Dad possessed a knack for finding water and then finding fish in that water.

The day in question played out like most summer weekend days of that time-period. My Dad and I went out fishing in one of our favorite ponds in Rhode Island. Bob always displayed his fishing license, oftentimes pinned to his sun hat or at other times pinned to his shirt. I know that my father felt proud to be a fisherman, and he wanted to display the fact that he was. On the other hand, I usually kept my license in my tackle-box amid an assortment of artificial lures. We rarely used live bait, as we felt that it was more challenging to catch fish with lures. Truth be told now, I never liked to put a worm on a hook, and I definitely didn't like hooking other types of live bait, either.

Sometimes my Mom, Dad, and I would sit three in our canoe and go fishing, but on this occasion, just my Dad and I went. My Mom or I would usually do most of the paddling. That day I did most of the work. We'd move about here and there while launching casts. Each cast was executed with care, as it could result in the catch of a lifetime. I'd learned to use a spinning-reel at a very young age. My Dad had once mentioned that he'd learned to fish on a hand-line, and he'd even talk about that primitive fishing-gear with enthusiasm. The technology in fishing had come a long way, and I for one happily employed the new high-tech reels. They made casting a true joy, and we developed our accuracy to an amazing level. We could hit a spot one square inch in size while avoiding trees, underbrush, and weeds in the process.

Rhode Island is a pretty state. The ponds that we'd usually fish in were tree lined. The water was crystal clear. Clean air filled our lungs; there was no trash to be seen. We were often the only canoe on a given pond, so it was quiet and peaceful. Getting to the ponds involved just a short drive, as Rhode Island is the smallest state. The natural settings that we enjoyed further enhanced our trips.

"Ray, see that swirl over there!" My Dad shouted excitedly.

"Get your line in. I'm switching to a rubber worm. It was big. Did you see it?"

"Yeah," I said, but I only saw the ripples after the fact. My Dad had actually seen part of the fish's body breaking the surface.

Whenever my Dad saw any splash, he'd jump with excitement. Fish triggered an automatic response in him. He was happy at moments like that and then nothing else in the world seemed to matter. Pure joy is the best way to describe those times.

"Don't rock the canoe, Dad," I said, as waves moved off from the bow. He was busy pulling a worm out of his tackle box.

I usually sat in the back of the canoe because I was the better canoeist. My position in the stern made it easier for me to steer the narrow boat. Being up front gave my Dad a small advantage too when it came to casting. I didn't mind. I probably enjoyed it more when he caught a fish than when I caught one myself. His happiness was profound.

"What size hook do you think I should use?" my Dad asked.

Even though such questions were rhetorical, I would respond,

"Maybe a size six?"

"Always sharpen your hooks," he'd say while filing.

Sometimes I thought that his meticulous preparations delayed him getting a line in the water, but I never mentioned that. He sure did enjoy the process. In my roughly fifty years of fishing, my father was one of the few fishermen that I ever fished with who always sharpened his hooks, including brand-new hooks.

"The hooks have to be sharp. You don't want to lose a fish because you didn't sharpen a hook."

"You're right," I responded, agreeing with him.

"Anything?"

"No, I think it was just a Pickerel."

"Okay, let's move to a new spot," Bob said after it seemed clear that this fish had swum away.

Usually in the heat of the battle, my Dad seemed to be changing lures or sharpening hooks. Maybe he was performing this sort of activity when we saw fish in order to give me a better chance to catch them. We both usually caught our fair share, though. When fishing for Trout, we would often reach our limit. Fish which we didn't plan to eat, we would carefully release. They'd grow larger, and we'd certainly be back. We always felt that we'd be able to return to our favorite spots forever. There wasn't ever a sense of our time together ending.

Our focus zoomed in on the fishing. We didn't talk much besides fishing, but that was okay, since being together is what was important to both of us. On such trips we were true companions. Our opinions mattered equally. We shared time; we shared our lives. On these trips we'd spend hours and hours together.

"You hungry?" I'd always be the first to pose that question. Due to his keen focus on fishing, my Dad might not have eaten if I hadn't been along.

His concentration on fishing let him pass time very quickly. Hunger was secondary.

"Yes; pass me a sandwich."

The cooler containing our food would usually be back near my end of the canoe since I liked to snack throughout our time on the water.

"What did Roxy pack today? Oh, Tuna fish with lettuce."

"I have a couple of baloney and cheese, and one peanut-butter and jelly. Here's your water."

I would stretch out my legs and relax during our lunches. On a clear day I liked to feel the sun on my face. We often fished with our shirts off and enjoyed the sun's rays. That day cool temperatures kept our jackets on. It felt peaceful floating on the water with my Dad. I felt no worries. While on the water fishing, we were content. I am so thankful that Bob found peace on the water, while pursuing his favorite hobby. Being out in nature together was a great joy. Our minds weren't cluttered with current events, and the bad things that were taking place in the world. At times like this one, we lived in bless. Content and happy.

Situated between us, but within arm's length of each of us and against the side of the canoe, rested an aluminum net. The lightweight, silver-colored net had a green, nylon mesh attached to its circular end. The butt of the net was covered by a small, yellow-plastic cap. We perfected our netting technique over the years, so as not to tangle our lines and hooks in the nylon, while bringing a catch on board. Typically, we netted only big fish. We hadn't made use of the net yet that day.

"I have to take a leak," my Dad proclaimed in a voice that indicated he meant a few minutes ago. The water had gone through him quickly. And, on his doctor's advice he drank about eight glasses of water per day.

"Okay, I'll bring us ashore on that beach over there where those geese are."

After lunch my Dad usually needed to pee before I did. He always used the word "leak." He never said, "I have to pee," "I need to piss," or "I have to go potty." I could stand up and pee over the side of the canoe, but my Dad didn't like to do this. Although he'd been around water all of his life, he didn't like to go swimming. The thought of capsizing the canoe horrified him. We carried extra fishing-poles, camera, anchor, spare paddle, gaff, towels, pail, knife, cooler, sunblock, and other gear. Successfully retrieving all of that equipment after flipping over would've been difficult, not to mention the discomfort of driving home in soaking-wet clothing.

I felt an urge coming on to pee also, so I quickened my rate of paddling.

"Here we go," I said, as I beached the front end of the canoe on the brown sandy beach.

"Look at those geese, big things," my Dad said, seemingly a little bit concerned.

"Hold the boat while I get out. Thanks," I said.

With the last half of my P-and-J sandwich in hand, I jumped onto the shore beside my Dad, and then using my other hand gripped my Dad's canoe seat and dragged the boat up on the shore a few feet farther. The boat was now secure.

We looked around and, seeing no one, my Dad walked over near a bush, undid his zipper, pulled down his underwear, and began to pee. The geese hovered surprisingly close by; these big birds weren't intimidated by us. Maybe they had a nest nearby. My Dad peed up a storm, and a steady flow of almost-clear liquid splashed on the shore. At that point I saw an opportunity. I broke off several small pieces of bread from my half-sandwich and tossed them a couple of feet in front of my Dad.

The crumbs landed between Bob and the geese. Several large geese moved in to take the bait.

"Ray, Ray!" my Dad shouted, while flailing and nearly falling over backward.

I tossed a few more pieces of bread with great precision. My Dad's laughter only served to increase an already steady flow, and he was unable to switch off his valve. The largest of the geese rapidly approached the source of the liquid's flow.

"Get out of here!" my Dad shouted between laughs.

"Raaaaaayyyyyyyyyy!!!"

I doubled over with uncontrollable laughter, and, of course, was no help at all in repelling the angry geese. One huge white goose lunged at my Dad's private part, but gripped only trousers in its orangey beak, as my Dad had been too quick after all. He swatted at the beast, and eventually it reluctantly retreated. It made one more futile charge. Bob repackaged his equipment and quickly zipped up. There was a splash spot on his trousers, as he didn't bother to shake off. The goose didn't allow it.

Bob and I laughed ourselves silly, as we launched the boat while still under attack. The lunging orangey beaks were missing us, but not at all by a comfortable distance. I reached safety first, as I worked my way to the back of the boat. I grabbed my oar, and assisted Bob, as he gave us a strong push off. While the angry geese snapped at his hands, we made our retreat. I turned the boat around, and my Dad faced the center of the pond. As we hurriedly paddled away to return to safety and the calm pond waters, I glanced back at the angry geese who seemed to be reclaiming the beach for themselves. Their squawking remained audile for a while.

"Whew, that was close," I gasped with a big smile on my face.

My Dad simply shook his head from side-to-side and reached for a towel to dry himself off.

Chapter 2
Largemouth Bass

My Dad often proclaimed, "The next person to catch a world-record Largemouth Bass will make millions." And even though the Rhode Island state record for Largemouth Bass fell more than twenty pounds short of the world record, in those days we'd always dream about hooking the record-breaking monster. Twenty pounds might not sound like much, but the record fish caught in 1932 in the Deep South weighed three times as much as the Rhode Island state-record fish. Fish grow all year round in Georgia, but only half the year in Rhode Island. I'm not sure why the Rhode Island fish weighed only one-third instead of one half of what the Georgia fish did. I should've asked my Dad. Just like a lottery-ticket buyer we held out hope and the belief that we might land "The Big One." We were dreamers.

One day while out canoeing on the Wood River, I discovered a bend in the river having a deep undercut. The murky water in the pool sank down nearly ten-feet deep in one corner. The average depth of the water in this section of the river measured only three or four feet, so this spot provided the coolest water in the river. I caught five or six Largemouth Bass in this hole the first time that I fished it. When I returned home and told my Dad about the trip, he seemed eager to go back to that very place with me. He felt certain that a big Bass still lurked in that deep pool. I could see his excitement.

In fishing circles there's a well-known video which shows a Largemouth Bass striking and consuming a swimming duck. As the name implies, Largemouth Bass do have (very) large mouths. The mouth of an eight-to-ten-pound Largemouth Bass can accommodate a softball. We always dreamed about catching a trophy Largemouth Bass of that size. Both my Dad and I had caught Largemouth Bass just over six pounds, but nothing bigger. Maybe the newfound spot in the Wood River would prove to be the place.

It wasn't long before my Dad and I embarked on a fishing-trip to the Wood River destined for the location with the high potential. The scenery appeared pleasant with lush green trees, colorful flowers, and delicate butterflies hovering in mid-air. Dragonflies with transparent wings zoomed here and there, and occasionally landed on the canoe. Places where we would normally have fished along the riverbanks would have to wait until our return trip later in the day, if we fished in them at all. On that day we were headed directly for the bend where the deep pocket of cool water stood. We paddled vigorously. Occasionally, my Dad would ask how much farther. I felt sure that we would arrive at our stopping point before long. I played a mental video of me reeling in a monster-sized Bass. For us the tension built.

"What are you going to use?" my Dad asked.

"I'm going with my little black Rebel."

My favorite lure during those times was called a Rebel. I used one of the smaller Rebels, which measured only about three inches long. The lure sported two medium-sized treble hooks. A protruding well-angled, clear-plastic beak forced the lure underwater when it was pulled. After years of practice, I made the lure look like a wounded Shiner by employing well-timed, jerky movements of my wrists and twitches to the tip of my fishing-pole. Shiners are silver-colored fish, and they're one of the favorite foods of Largemouth Bass. I felt confident that I could attract and hook a big Largemouth Bass with my Rebel.

"Did you sharpen your hooks?"

"Yeah," I replied, although I didn't really remember for sure if I had. My Dad always asked that question. Always. He loved the preparation that went into fishing.

"We should've bought some Shiners," my Dad said. He was now regretting not having spent a few dollars for live bait. Although I made the Rebel look like a shiner, it certainly didn't smell like a Shiner or feel like a Shiner when bitten.

"Are you going with a worm?"

"Yes; I'm using a nine-inch black worm with a propeller tail. It's weedless, the way I hook it. I'm using a weighted hook, so that I can get the worm down to the bottom."

"Good idea."

My Dad loved to illustrate fishing-techniques to others, for example, how to hook a worm to make it weedless, how to tie the improved-clinch knot, or how to attach a bobber to a piece of fishing-line. At last it looked to me as if we'd arrived.

"Okay, we're coming up on the spot. Slow down," I said. "Be quiet."

Thank goodness we arrived to find the spot empty of other fishermen. We maneuvered the canoe carefully and quietly, so as not to disturb any fish in the area. I backed my end of the canoe into some tall grass, and we grabbed our fishing-poles with great anticipation. The grass served to anchor us. We'd probably be here a while. At least until we were certain that The Big One wasn't going to bite or we'd hooked him.

We cast our lures with precision. Our casts seemed choreographed, but we never really spoke about where we'd cast. Each of us knew the other's habits. Instinctively, we avoided each other's line, but it was more than that. Like two mine-sweepers clearing a field, we swept our lures over each inch of the pool. Our mathematical minds made sure that we used the minimum number of casts to achieve this coverage. We talked little. Genetics and togetherness allowed us to co-ordinate effortlessly.

When I would cast, I needed to be carefully not to hook my Rebel on one of the branches behind me. Just beyond where the canoe was backed up in the grass, there were some overhanging branches. I was whipping my pole in a violent motion to hit the desired locations in the pool with my Rebel. Had I snagged a branch, the hooks on the Rebel would have been deeply implanted there. Not to mention that I would risk an injury to one of my shoulders or my wrists from the sudden unexpected resistance. I didn't falter.

On that day two- and three-pound Largemouth Bass seemed unimportant. We each caught our share of those, and we released them. Our intuition told us unequivocally that a monster lurked in this hole. The questions of who would catch it and when preoccupied our minds. Although we never voiced many ideas or opinions, I suppose that we often thought about the same things while fishing. I knew for certain on that day that we both were dreaming of hooking The Big One.

My mother had packed us a lunch as usual, but we delayed eating. After we caught The Big One, we'd eat, but not before. For a while the fishing had quieted down. Neither one of us had caught anything for a spell. I'd repositioned the canoe several times. Now the narrow boat was situated among some fallen trees. The current in the river didn't move us because the branches pressing up against the sides of the boat acted as braces. I placed a perfect cast, and my Rebel landed two inches from the river's high grassy bank.

Casting felt fun. I cocked open the bail with my left hand, held the line with my right index finger, and whipped the pole backward. As three feet of line outstretched from the tip of the pole, I would feel the Rebel at a maximum distance behind me. At precisely that moment a quick and elegant forward whipping motion sent the Rebel on an upward arching missile-like flight. I enjoyed the whipping sound. The lure landed tail first, after having traveled in a looping semicircle. Its entry sounded quietly, and the lightweight lure left only small rings in the water. I would instinctively close the bail with a quick turn of the reel's handle. That way, if a fish struck the lure immediately, I was ready to set the hook.

"See that wa-wa-wave," I stuttered while trying to get out a few words.

A ten-inch wave had formed immediately after the Rebel had landed; no doubt whatsoever: The Big One swam toward my lure. At that moment excitement overwhelmed me, and I seemed incapable of speech. I wanted and needed to tell my Dad what was happening, but he'd find out soon enough. We'd been anticipating this moment. Wham! The big kahuna hit my Rebel. Swoosh! A huge splash resulted, and now my Dad pivoted quickly and saw what was happening.

"Set the hook! Set the hook, Ray!" he exclaimed.

"I have 'im, Dad! It's The Big One!"

"Set the hook! Set it!"

My father quickly reeled in his line to get it out of my way. He set his pole down in the canoe are attaching the rubber one to one of the pole's eyelets. My Dad was always thinking. He'd probably already gone over this scenario in his mind. We both focused on the upcoming fight. The big fish pulled out line. The reel made a high-pitched hissing noise.

"He's running. Tighten the drag! Tighten the drag!"

"All he wants is line."

"Don't let him run too far."

I cinched down the drag a little. The fishing-hole's dimensions were smaller than an Olympic-sized swimming-pool, so I knew that the Largemouth couldn't get too far—unless he swam up- or downstream that is. The fish made a strong dash for survival.

"You got 'im? What a monster. Look at that splash!"

The fish beat its tail one last time on the surface making a statement to us and then dove. My pole bent significantly. The thin tip appeared near its breaking-point. My mind told me that my light fishing-line might break at any second. The tension of the line in the water caused small ripples to form along its edges. You could hear a zippy noise emanating from the line where it touched the water. I felt that the line would snap any second.

"Hold the tip up, Ray!" my Dad reminded me.

My Dad's advice flowed freely. He coached me. The action heated up, and I did what I could to follow his instructions. He taught me how to fish; he was the Master. I did what I could by everything was happening very quickly, hours of waiting for these few tense minutes.

I battled the fish. We'd been sunning ourselves, and with my T-shirt off I noticed the muscles in my arms and my chest flexed fully and tensely. I felt sweat dripping off me. This fish didn't want to be caught. I struggled. My Dad reached for the net. I felt fatigue in my arms. My adrenaline took over. The canoe rocked. Waves formed in the pool. The boat didn't move much.

"Steady. Steady now. Hold it."

"Where is he?"

"I think he's gone under the canoe."

"Oh, no, no, no!"

"No!" one of us shouted.

The war continued. Although the battle had taken only five or six minutes, my adrenaline supplies were depleted. I would need to rely on my conditioning for the remainder of the fight. Maybe the sun had drained me. God, we should have eaten lunch. My energy vanished due to my overly excited state.

"Take it easy. Take it easy! Slow down!"

The fish no longer pulled out any line. The hissing noise of the drag subsided. I'd won this phase of the fight. Gradually, I reeled The Big One toward my side of the canoe. I felt him coming toward me. Was I about to win the battle? I couldn't wait to see him. To see The Big One caught and in our cooler.

"Get the net ready! Net!" I yelled.

"Do you have the net ready?" I quickly asked to see if my earlier command had been followed. Later my question seemed silly, as, of course, I knew that my Dad awaited netting this monster. Bob may have been more attentive to the situation than I was. He peered intensely into the water where he thought the fish would first break the surface. I could see drops of sweat falling off of my Dad, as he clutched the net tightly in both hands.

"He's diving!"

"Don't let him get near those branches! You'll never get him out of there, Ray!"

Suddenly my dream of pulling in this giant seemed to be fading fast. The fish was more intelligent than I'd anticipated. He was seeking refuge amount the branches, and surely my lightweight and stressed line would easily snap if wrap around a limb.

"No!"

"Get him away from those branches. He'll wrap your line around a stump and snap it. Ray, keep the tip up! Higher!"

We looked at each other dejectedly, as my line disappeared into the tangle of limbs. The tension in the line eased up, and there were no longer ripples emanating from alongside where the line entered the water. In other words the line was no longer taut. The Big One appeared to have won this round.

"Well, good fight. You lost him," my Dad said sadly and with compassion. His head hung low.

I could no longer feel any tension on my line. The tip of the rod no longer bent downward. I knew that my Dad was right, but I couldn't give up just yet. We waited and waited, but I felt nothing. After a few more minutes of waiting, I asked for the net. The Big One may have already fled the area, but I was going to make one, last-ditch effort.

"Thanks. I'm going to jam the net down there and see what happens."

My father's reaction indicated that he felt the situation was hopeless. I could see that he'd already given up any hope of me landing The Big One. As I pushed the head of the net below the surface, I quickly saw that this idea was doomed to failure because the nylon instantly became stuck in the branches. I groped for an answer. My desire to land The Big One still overpowered me. I still thought that he might be on the Rebel. On the other hand, in all likelihood he had swam from the area and had wrapped my line around my stump, as my Dad had thought.

"Here, take the net back. I'm going to use my paddle. Keep the net ready just in case," I said with a modicum of hope.

I picked up the worn wooden paddle in my left hand, and held my fishing-pole in my right hand. I'd reeled up the line, so that it remained taut. At first I gently pressed the paddle among the branches. Then out of frustration, I violently began jamming it into the morass. My situation was hopeless. Time was running out. My hope ebbed. I stabbed at the branches, creating turbulence in the water. I kept stabbing with the paddle. Miraculously, I felt a tug on the line. The pole bent down further.

"I felt him, Dad!" I said with wild excitement.

"He's still hooked?"

"I think so!"

The fish broke loose from the tree limbs, and my line came free. My Rebel was still in The Big One's mouth. He'd hidden in the limbs to test my resolve, hoping that I'd give up. Now the clever fish swam out of the morass. I must've hit him on the back with the paddle. A feeling that he obviously didn't enjoy and didn't want to endure any longer.

"Net him. Net him. Net him!" I commanded.

My father abruptly shifted his position in the canoe. My Dad reached out and scooped up the behemoth using the textbook netting-technique. The metal handle of the net bent under the weight of The Big One. The green nylon stretched to its limit. I could see that we were about to lose him for good. Our net wasn't rated for a fish this heavy. Oh, no, don't lose him now after this great struggle, I thought. Please, God.

"Bring him into the boat. Into the boat!" I shouted trying to will the fish into the canoe.

My Dad swung the net over the center of the canoe. We both stared agape, as The Big One flopped on the bottom of the canoe. We'd caught

The Big One together. He was now in our possession.

"I thought you'd lost him. Great job!"

"Thanks, Dad. Sorry I yelled at you."

We took some happy pictures of The Big One, washed our hands, and wolfed down our late lunch. Looking back, I don't really remember much else from that day. I only recall that my Dad's joy and amazement seemed the same as it would have been if *he* had landed The Big One. He might have even been happier that I'd caught the huge fish. I know that he was proud of me for not having given up the fight, even when it looked certain that I'd lost The Big One. In the years that followed we often talk about the day that we'd teamed up to catch The Big One.

Chapter 3
World-Record Eel

My Dad wanted to immortalize himself in some way, and he did that through his children, his Scrimshaw, and his fishing. I knew that he had a great fear of dying. Creating permanence in one form or another seemed to help ease his fear. My two sisters' and brother's families have combined for six grandchildren. And, my brother's two boys would carry on the Greenlaw name. My Dad's Scrimshaw, etchings of whaling and shipping scenes on whale's teeth, can be found in homes and in art galleries throughout New England. He signed his artwork with the moniker "Bob" in tiny letters. As for his fishing, what better way to immortalize himself in fishing than by setting a world record? His name would literally go down in the books.

Rhode Island waters in particular and New England waters in general aren't known for producing giant fish. The cold winters prevent the fish from growing as large as they do in warmer climes. Nevertheless, Rhode Island waters have yielded world-record fish, including for example, Pickerel. Both my Dad and I'd approached catching world-record-sized Pickerel in the Wood River. Our catches tipped the scales at just over six pounds, and those fish had gigantic teeth. My Dad seemed to be afraid of getting bitten by such a large Pickerel. I always figured that as a child he must have had a bad experience with a big Pickerel.

Bob took a scientific approach to most things. His training in mathematics, in seismology, and in nuclear engineering carried over to fishing. He left few details to chance—always making sure that each reel contained precisely the correct amount of line, that each point and barb on every treble hook had been sharpened, and that he carried with him depth-charts for wherever we were fishing. Careful preparation is important, but setting a world record requires more than just preparation of equipment. Knowledge, technique, and desire are critical ingredients, too. Also required is Fisherman's Luck.

My Dad wanted to set a world record, so he studied the record books. My father knew the types of fish which lived in the different ponds in New England. He knew which ponds contained big fish. He often talked about landing a huge Perch.

"Ray, there are big White Perch in Worden's Pond," he would say with great excitement. "I think we may be able to set a world record in the six-pound-line category."

Fishing world records don't depend solely on the weight of the fish. The strength of the fishing-line is also taken into account. The records are kept in line categories such as the two-pound class, four-pound class, six-pound class, and so on, but the gaps get larger, for example, 60-pound class, 80-pound class, and 100-pound class. Interestingly, on a fishing-line rated to any class x, a fish much larger than x pounds can be caught. For example, on 100-pound-class line, it is possible to land a 500-pound Tuna. My Dad's world record would probably come from a lightweight-line category given his locale. If he'd lived somewhere else, his record would have come from a correspondingly appropriate category.

From time-to-time we would catch a near world-record fish—a huge Bluegill, meaning just over a pound-and-a-half, or an enormous Yellow Perch, again weighing about a pound-and-a-half. Such catches would motivate my Dad to try to break a world record in these categories, and for weeks he would talk only about Bluegills or about Yellow Perch. Eventually, his enthusiasm would switch over to another type of fish: Smallmouth Bass, Carp, Pike, or one of the many species of Trout.

Bob made many preparations and learned a great deal about the procedures involved in setting a fishing world record. Obviously, one can't just show up at a Bass Pro Shop and inform them that "I just broke the world record for Largemouth Bass in the eight-pound-line category. I released the 35-pound beast at the insistence of my wife." With such an outlandish claim one would be laughed out of the store by the employees. Fisherman tell tales, so proof of catch is actually required. There's no honor system among fishermen.

A fisherman intent on breaking a world record must carry with him an accurate scale to weigh candidate fish, must be able to identify fish species, must be familiar with the records in the various categories, and must know the line class that he is using. A witness must be present who can verify that the fish was caught in the manner claimed. A potential-record fish must be taken to an authorized bait-shop where the fish can be accurately weighed. Two disinterested people must witness the weighing on a certified scale. The first 25 feet of fishing-line from the reel on which the fish was caught must be provided, and that line needs to be calibrated and confirmed to be of a particular category by a certified lab. The lab conducts five separate tests on the line and computes an average strength. The fish must be caught in eligible waters during the legal fishing-season. A professional fisheries person must identify a catch's species, photos must be taken of the catch, and a notary public must notarize the application form for a world-record fish.

Some manufacturers' 4-pound-class fishing-line is actually rated, for example, as 5.5-pound-class line when calibrated in a lab. This fact makes the average fisherman believe that the line quality is higher than it is. Imagine 4-pound-class line having the strength of 5.5-pound-class line. Well, if it has the strength of 5.5-pound-class line, it's 6-pound-class line, not 4-pound-class line. As one delves into the details of setting a world record, it becomes clear that quite a bit of effort is involved. For Bob this effort felt like nothing. My Dad handled details with ease. His facility with details rubbed off on me and served me well in my life and career.

Bob simultaneously held fishing licenses for many different states. He always possessed Rhode Island and Massachusetts licenses, and at various times licenses for Alaska, California, Connecticut, Florida, Georgia, Maine, New Hampshire, and Washington. My Dad collected many things besides fishing licenses. He collected guns, knives, minerals, ivory carvings, beads, antiques, magazines, books, tools, and, of course, fishing-gear. To my mother's dismay, Bob rarely threw anything away. Everything was extremely well organized and clean. He'd clean the guns in his gun collection on a schedule each year. He always washed off his fishing gear after each outing.

My Dad kept his fishing-gear in the basement of my parents' home. The volume of his gear required a large space to store. The basement was his man cave. He'd built two, fishing-pole racks which hung from the basement ceiling. These racks accommodated his dozen or so fishing-poles. Each pole was outfitted with a top-of-the-line fishing-reel. Bob also kept spare reels. A chest-high cabinet with a couple dozen deep drawers contained every type of fishing-lure ever manufactured: Jitterbugs, spinners, rubber worms, Hula poppers, plugs, Hawaiian wigglers, and so on. When opening any drawer, one felt struck by the beautiful colors of all of the lures. There were hooks of every size and shape, weights of every magnitude between an eighth of an ounce up to several ounces, bobbers of every bright two-tone color combination and size, and spools of line of every weight class. The basement could have served effectively as a small bait-shop sans live bait.

My Dad loved to organize his things. He was a fanatic with plastic containers. Bob possessed every conceivable-sized plastic box, and among his boxes existed every conceivable partitioning of the space. These different configurations allowed him to pack up any assortment of a dozen or so lures, and give each one its own separate home in the plastic container. Using this technique, no lures ever became tangled. Of course, my Dad owned three or four large tackle-boxes, and several small ones, too. Each of the boxes overflowed with colorful lures. Amazingly, my Dad knew exactly where every item was housed. He *never* misplaced any gear.

My mother Roxy accompanied my father on thousands of fishing-trips. When we kids were working, out on dates, or off at college, Roxy went along. After all of their children had moved out of the house, my mother would take their place as "crew" for my Dad's fishing expeditions. Whenever my Dad wanted to go fishing, Roxy went along. She always made the best of the situation and was very patient in paddling my Dad around, while he searched for that world-record fish. Roxy traveled all over the country with my Dad on fishing-trips. My mother rarely fished.

With all the talk about a world-record Perch or Bluegill, I found it somewhat odd that the first world record my Dad set was for, of all things, an American Eel. Freshwater Eels are notoriously ugly. They are brownish, blackish, greenish, snake-looking creatures. Their faces look too small for their bodies. Eels are slimy and thin. My Dad caught a two-pound, one-ounce American Eel on four-pound-class line. Since I wasn't there, I can only imagine him reeling the Eel in:

"Roxy, I have something big here! Look at the line go out. Look at the tip of my fishing-pole. Get the net ready. Is it ready, Roxy?"

I can imagine my mother scrambling for the net after setting her book down. Then, with net in hand waiting for my Dad's catch to be brought alongside the canoe.

"It's pulling like an Eel, but it's too big. Is the net ready? Here it comes. Get ready. It's an Eel, a big one. Net it, Roxy! Roxxxyyyyy!"

"Bob!"

"Ha, ha," my Dad laughing.

"Let it go."

"This could be a world record."

"Bob!"

"We need to bring this one to the bait-shop."

And so, I'm sure that my mother patiently spent the remaining part of that day accompanying my father to the bait-shop, and carrying out the required steps for a world-record submission. I remember receiving in 1988 a copy of my Dad's certificate stating that he had attained a "World Record Angling Achievement." The American Eel was caught on June 28, 1988, in Dunham Pond, Massachusetts. Receiving that certificate was a proud moment for my Dad. When I received my copy of his certificate, I felt proud, too. My Dad was the only world-record holder whom I knew.

On February 18, 2000, my Dad broke the world record for catching a one-pound, fourteen-ounce Shortnose Gar on six-pound-class line. He caught that Gar in Cemetery Lake, Florida. When I received my copy of his certificate, I felt equally proud. Setting two world records in two states in two separate decades, and for two different species, was indeed an incredible angling achievement. In my eyes they solidified my Dad's place among the fishing greats.

Chapter 4
Hooked Fisherman

Bob grew up during the time of the Great Depression in the United States. He attended Clark University in Worcester, Massachusetts, and there he received an undergraduate degree in mathematics after four years of study. I remember my Dad teaching me Calculus when I was only twelve years old. He enjoyed sharing his knowledge about all subjects with me, and he possessed a great thirst for learning, which rubbed off on me. Bob seemed like a serious person to all my friends, but as this next story reveals, he did have a lighter side and a great sense of humor. He was a funny man. Few people ever saw that side of my father though. Perhaps if he'd grown up in less serious times, he'd have worried less about life.

Over the course of his career my father worked his way up from a junior underwriter to the level of Vice President at a major insurance company. However, truth be told, he was never a sharp dresser. In fact, my Dad watched each and every penny that he spent on clothing. He possessed a keen eye for sales and studied the newspaper ads at great length to locate good sales. Financially, he didn't need to be so thrifty, but his upbringing had taught him how to handle money carefully, and I for one believe that it's better to live within one's means than outside of them.

My Dad's obsession with saving a few dollars often corrupted his judgment when it came to purchasing clothing. His mania for a bargain and for sales forced him to drive all over New England in search of a great purchase. When he thought that he'd made a good deal, it gave him great satisfaction. Bob would buy winter clothing in the summer, and summer clothing in the winter. His dresser burst full of unused and unopened garments, likely obtained at three-for-one sales or something similar. Whenever I went to visit my father, he always gave me clothing. Always. I graciously accepted, but, in all honesty, some of the gifts didn't suit my style. They may not have really suited anyone's style which is why these items were being sold at rock-bottom prices.

The price of a piece of clothing on sale is directly proportional to the distastefulness of its color—for example, bright lime-green pants made of even the most expensive fabric cost less than normal blue jeans. My Dad would say to me "Ray, I bought these shirts on sale, three for ten dollars." It may have been a good buy, but as far as I was concerned, at least two of the three shirts were unwearable. Naturally, I never mentioned that fact to my Dad, as I wouldn't have wanted to hurt his feelings.

My Dad often bought dress slacks on sale. Again, the oddest color combinations are what remained on the racks the longest, their prices eventually dipping to my Dad's standards for purchase. Despite the fact that many pairs of my Dad's pants were dressy, the meager price that my Dad had paid for them allowed him to wear them fishing. On the particular day in question, my Dad wore a pair of strangely-colored, Johnny Hagar dress slacks. To the best of my recollection, the slacks had a plaid-like pattern, which consisted of at least six colors; the pants were made out of a polyester-type fabric. On his torso my Dad wore a single-colored, light-brown, golf shirt. I've no idea what I was wearing. I usually wore cutoffs and a T-shirt, and it probably didn't look like we came from the same family.

My Dad and I'd paddled the canoe to a promising-looking spot among several patches of green lily pads. Large white flowers with yellow centers protruded occasionally from among the plate-shaped pads. Little green frogs jumped from pad-to-pad; insects buzzed around happily; water bugs fought their way through the thick growth. We cast our lures in all directions, enjoying the day on the water. While fishing together, we felt free. The act of reeling in a lure was so practiced and natural to us that we did it effortlessly for hours.

That day we hadn't landed our usual haul of fish, yet. Then suddenly my Dad's fishing rod bent over dramatically. I saw his arms go taut, and his posture change. He perked up dramatically.

"I've got something big here, Ray!"

Our silence had been broken, as it typically was, when one of us hooked a fish. We'd wait for hours for moments like this one. When it came to fishing, we were both extremely patient people.

Stirred from my meditation, I said, "I'll get my line out of your way. Try to keep 'im out of the weeds!"

"Probably a Pickerel. Big one!"

After a minute or so of battling what we still thought was a Pickerel, Bob appeared to be winning the fight. He looked funny fishing in those dress slacks. He must've been extremely hot in the sun.

"Bring him a little closer, and I'll net him."

As the fish was drawn closer to the canoe through my Dad's skilled efforts, it became clear that the fish was indeed a Pickerel. We rarely ate Pickerel, unless they were huge. Pickerel are extremely thin and bony fish, and we much preferred eating Largemouth Bass or White Perch. We ate a lot of fish when I was growing up. In fact, we ate fish four or five nights every week. My mother often dipped the fish in flour swishing it around loosely in a brown-paper bag and then fried the fish in butter. To this day I prefer fish exactly the way my mother used to prepare it. No special sauces for me. I actually enjoy the taste of fresh fish itself.

"I think that I can just lift him into the canoe. Don't bother with the net."

The fish turned out to be a bit smaller than we'd initially thought. My Dad cared little if he lost this Pickerel, as we planned to release him anyway. Pickerel were feisty beasts and taking the hook out of a Pickerel's mouth was no easy feat. Pickerel have long sharp teeth.

"Sure?"

"Yes."

"Okay," I said returning the net to its home.

My Dad didn't want to get the energetic fish all tangled up in the green nylon of the net. He thought it would be an easy proposition to simply lift the fish into the canoe. There'd be little to no chance of his line snapping.

As Bob raised himself slightly out of his seat for better leverage, he simultaneously began to lift the Pickerel above the water toward the canoe. The Pickerel wiggled vigorously in a last-ditch, mid-air effort to shake itself loose from my father's lure, which by the way was a medium-sized blue-and-white Rebel having two treble hooks. I watched the Pickerel struggling valiantly; I was sure that it'd lost the battle. It fought on though and splashed about. At this stage of the game, my Dad rarely made a mistake. While watching my Dad's fishing-pole bending significantly, I saw a splash below and heard a sudden whipping sound. Whoosh! The Pickerel had vanished. Then I heard a scream. A scream that indicated my Dad was in a significant amount of pain.

"Shit!"

"What happened?" I inquired. I rarely heard my Dad swear.

"The hook; it's in past the barb!"

While sitting ten feet away in the back of the boat, I saw that blood dripped from my Dad's displayed thumb. The tension stored in the fishing-pole had rocketed my Dad's Rebel into his thumb, as the Pickerel had found its freedom. The swoosh that I'd heard was the Rebel traveling toward my Dad's thumb at high velocity. As my Dad had been leaning over and reaching out with his pole, his thumb had presented itself as a target.

"Look; it's in past the barb!" my Dad said again while holding his hurting hand up higher. Bob's face displayed a well-formed expression of disgust and embarrassment. He was in a lot of pain.

The situation didn't look good for my Dad's thumb. I thought the digit might swell and get infected. I hoped that his tetanus shot was up-to-date. Knowing my Dad, I was pretty certain that it was. He was a fanatic when it came to help issues.

"Cut the line," I instructed.

I could see that the bent over pole was pulling the lure even deeper into his bloody thumb. The tension on the line was significant. By now the pickerel that had been on my Dad's hook was long gone.

"With what? Do you have a knife?"

"No! I'll get that one out of your tackle-box for you."

Once I stood up and began working my way forward, the canoe rocked. With each step I took, no matter how carefully I moved, the barb went deeper into my Dad's thumb. I couldn't avoid jostling the canoe from side-to-side. Only about three or four feet of line was out from the tip of the pole. For some reason at that time neither one of us thought for him to release the bail on this reel to relieve the tension in the line. Things just happened to quickly, and we, unfortunately, overlooked that way of relieving my Dad's pain.

"Go back, Ray. This is killing me. I'll get the knife out."

My Dad opened up his tackle-box, located a knife, and successfully cut his fishing-line near where the Rebel had been attached. The top of the pole sprung up. This operation allowed him to rest his fishing-pole against the side of the canoe. For the moment he appeared more comfortable. His stress-level decreased somewhat. I could see some bloody spots near where my Dad. I could see a piece of line dangling off of his thumb.

"Good job," I said while encouraging my Dad.

I saw from my Dad's facial expression that he felt a lot of pain. My movements caused him additional pain, so I just sat as motionless as possible. I could only render verbal assistance.

"What am I going to do?" Bob asked with despair.

"Can you take it out?"

"No; it's in past the barb. Look."

I stared at his uplifted red thumb again. The situation didn't look good, but I didn't share that thought. Even the short strand of line that remained tied to the Rebel had drops of blood on it. I thought about what to do. I couldn't come up with any good solutions to the problem.

"I guess you'll have to push the hook all the way through and then cut the barb off. Then you can pull the hook out."

"Ray!"

Although my Dad didn't like this suggestion, he couldn't think of any better action to take. He knew that he'd have to subject himself to immense pain in order to push the barb all the way through his thumb. He'd be cutting an as yet uncut part of his thumb. And, the barb wasn't small, so he need to create a wide deep wound.

"I'll need my pliers," he said dejectedly.

While my Dad reached down to retrieve his pliers, he exclaimed, "Shit!"

"What? What happened?"

"Ray, I hooked the other hook on my pants. Oh, Ray!"

For all practical purposes my Dad was hog-tied. He bent over now, not voluntarily, but because his ankle and thumb were handcuffed together by a four-inch Rebel. He could no longer sit up straight. His predicament had gone from bad to worse.

"Shit!"

Despite the graveness of the situation, I could feel that I might burst out laughing any moment. My Dad was a funny man, and this situation seemed funny for some reason, despite his pain. His mannerisms were funny to me, not as quirky as Woody Allen, but very funny. I tried desperately to keep it together. What could go wrong next, I wondered. I told myself not to burst out laughing; I could barely contain myself. My Dad couldn't move without hurting his thumb more. And, he certainly could sit upright.

"What am I going to do, Ray?" my Dad said in desperation.

"Can you get the pants off?"

I almost lost it. Bob moved a little. We both realized how ridiculous my suggestion was. Fortunately, my Dad began laughing before I did. He cracked up loudly, rocking the canoe. Then I let loose with a burst of laughter so great that the canoe shook steadily. We nearly capsized. More blood dripped from my Dad's thumb.

"Ouch, ouch!" my Dad exclaimed in between laughs.

"The hook is being driven in deeper."

The two of us couldn't get a grip on ourselves. My eyes teared up; so did my Dad's. I peed my pants; my Dad peed his. We laughed harder—him to relieve the stress, and, well, me, I found his predicament unthinkably hilarious. With one hand he'd undone the button on his pants, but bent over as he was, he was still essentially helpless.

"I think I'm going to have to cut the pants."

I knew that he wouldn't have suggested that except as a last resort. Good idea, I thought to myself. I also thought to myself that this cutting meant that he'd have to throw the pants away. I suppressed further laughter. I knew that he hated wasting or getting rid of anything.

"Can you reach the knife for me?"

I stood up, and immediately the canoe rocked. My hunched-back father who'd been bent over for at least ten minutes couldn't move. He looked like an animal caught in a tar pit—helpless and running out of energy. The sun beat down.

"Sit back down. I'll have to do this myself."

Somehow he managed to access the knife for a second time, although that movement caused him great pain. Then I saw him doubled-over hacking away at his slacks. I knew that the cutting was successful, when I saw a strip of the Johnny Hagar's dangling from the Rebel. My Dad sat upright at long last. Now there was a piece of fishing line and a piece of his pants hanging off of the Rebel on his thumb.

"Good going, Dad."

This time my Dad exercised a bit more caution in locating the pliers. I could see the red-handled, needle-nose pliers in his pain-free hand. My father yelped in pain as he used the pliers to push the barb all the way through his thumb. God, that must have hurt, I thought. He worked the pliers with his good hand and managed to cut off the barb which was now protruding from the other side of his thumb from where the hook had entered. I heard a small snap, as he succeeded. My Dad quickly pulled the hook back through his thumb in the opposite direction in which it had entered, and then tossed the Rebel with the strip of slacks and fishing line still attached to it into the bottom of the canoe. With that act he had freed himself.

Finally, I was able to get up to assist. The canoe rocked, as I grabbed a napkin from the cooler. When I reached for a Band-Aid from Bob's tackle-box, I noticed many droplets of blood in the bottom of the canoe. I wiped off his swollen and throbbing thumb with the white napkin, and the thin tissue quickly filled with blood. We applied pressure to the bleeding wound. Once my Dad's thumb was cleaned and dried, I covered it with a Band-Aid after applying some antibiotic cream. I'd fastened the Band-Aid too tightly in my haste, and I accidentally caused him additional pain.

"Sorry, Dad, sorry," I said with great feeling.

In a number of respects my Dad was a tough man. He didn't complain about the hooking incident for the remainder of the day. I did most of the paddling back to where we had parked the car, as his thumb still hurt significantly. I thought about the Pickerel that had escaped and about the Johnny Hagar slacks. I never saw either one of them again after that day. My Dad and I never spoke about this incident, but I suppose it brought a smile to both of our faces from time to time. He must have thought of it often because whenever he etched Scrimshaw he would be staring down at his scared thumb.

Chapter 5
Beautiful Rainbow Trout

When a typical fisherman thinks of big Rainbow Trout, the first U. S. state that pops into his mind isn't Rhode Island. However, Rhode Island has a very good stocking program. Each year when Trout season rolled around, my Dad was ready and eager to fish. I don't remember him missing an opening day. Bob usually caught some big Rainbows early in the season. He didn't fish so much with flies as he did with PowerBait. Bob never really got into fly fishing. He preferred to use a spinning reel which must've been a huge step up from his early days of hand lining and bait-casting reels.

In the fall season when I would return to college in Southern California and later to graduate school in Washington State, my Mom would go Trout-fishing with my Dad. Roxy always had her own fishing-license. Usually, she didn't fish, but her license doubled their catch limit. While fishing alone, my Dad often reached their combined limit. He loved to eat Rainbow Trout. My father would've eaten fish seven days a week if my Mom had let him. Certainly, Rainbow Trout was one of his favorite meals.

My Mom and Dad would give fish to less-fortunate people, not just those of lesser fishing-ability, but to people who truly needed the fish for food. These poor people could be found trying to catch a meal at some of our fishing haunts. None of them had a valid fishing license. My Dad would offer up a portion of his catch in a friendly and caring way, and people were always appreciative of his generosity. In this way my parents provided many meals to people in need. Many poor people recognized and remembered my Dad, and they would ask him for a portion of his catch. When he had extra, he always gave them some fish.

My Dad had fish-cleaning down to a science. He studied each fish species so that he knew exactly where all the bones lay. After meticulously sharpening his filleting knife, he would carve up a day's catch with great ease and precision. He spent hours teaching me how to clean a wide variety of species. My mother prepared fish in a simple yet delicious manner. Our family loved the taste of fresh fish, and we didn't use any condiments or tartar-sauce on our fish. To us dishes such as sweet-and-sour fish ruined the taste of the fresh fish. We never ate frozen fish. Our fish was always very fresh, and I suppose that if we did have to eat fish that wasn't fresh, then we might have preferred it to be doctored up in some way.

The fall is a beautiful time in New England and a beautiful time for fishing there. The cool crisp air and the fall foliage make drifting on a river in a canoe or floating on a pond a special experience. The oranges, yellows, and reds in the leaves paint tranquil scenes. On calm water the reflections double one's pleasure. My Dad loved to fish in the fall in Rhode Island. My Mom enjoyed accompanying my Dad. There were few insects around in the crisp air. Fall on a peaceful pond was a lovely experience.

Fishermen learn to identify fish merely by observing their wakes and splashes, and Rainbow Trout make a unique splash, while feeding on surface insects. When my Dad would see such a series of expanding rings, he would get especially excited.

"Roxy, did you see that?" he would ask in a loud voice.

"Where?" my Mom would say looking around.

"There!"

"Yes."

"Quick; row over there."

And my Mom would paddle the canoe to a spot where my Dad could cast into the center of the rings. They worked as a team, and they caught and ate many fish together. No matter how many times my Dad saw a splash from any fish, he got very excited. There was just something in his blood that made him want to fish. A swirl or a splash meant there was a creature lurking below the surface that he had a chance to catch.

Few Rainbow Trout caught in Rhode Island waters exceed two pounds. However, my Dad would use extremely lightweight tackle, and this meant that pulling in a two-pound fish was still challenging and fun. My Dad believed that fish had exceptional vision, and thus could see your line and avoid being caught. He always used the lightest class of line that seemed feasible. Of course, this required more skill since a fish could break the lightweight line much more easily. Due to his expert technique, Bob didn't lose too many lures over the years.

On the particular fall day in question, my Mom and Dad fished in the Wood River, one of my Dad's favorite places to catch Rainbow Trout in

Rhode Island. My Dad dressed in a gray flannel shirt with brown buttons; the shirt had a single large pocket. Around the front of his neck the top two buttons exposed a light-blue T-shirt. Bob's habit of wearing dress slacks while fishing had passed, and he wore a stylish olive-green pair of khakis from L. L. Bean. He looked more like an outdoorsman now than a golfer.

Bean's of Freeport, Maine, was one of my Dad's favorite sport shops in New England, but he shopped at them all—Thompson's, Kittery Trading Post, Eddie Bauer, REI, and K-mart, which, by the way, used to have an excellent selection of fishing gear. He liked to pick up gear, handle it, and see whether or not it felt right to him. Only, if it felt good in his hands and the price was right would he purchase a piece of gear. Bob never shopped online, which is just as well, since he loved to go into bait-shops and talk fishing with the proprietors and the clientele.

"What's biting?" "What are they hitting?" "Has anyone caught anything near the bridge?" My Dad could approach anyone and immediately begin querying them about fishing. We enjoyed watching his skillful approach to obtaining information regarding fishing. He engaged people, and his own shyness vanished. Bob's enthusiasm for fishing was contagious. I couldn't really have imagined him talking to most of the people whom he did, unless the topic was fishing. Somehow he was at ease talking with nearly anyone about fishing.

For the most part my Dad kept his hair short. I don't know if he merely liked it that way, if my Mom did, if this style had endured from his military days, or if Bob felt that he looked better with short hair due to his receded hair-line. He wore tri-focal glasses. My Dad could tie nearly any fishing knot, and knew them all. He would take off his glasses, squint, and somehow tie all types of knots with great precision. Some knots involved the equivalent of threading a needle multiple times. His extreme patience and scientific approach paid off. I knew that when I reached his age, I wouldn't be able to tie such knots with such ease anymore.

Having similar eyes to my Dad, as I've become older I can only now truly appreciate the skill and patience required of an elderly person with fading vision to tie such knots. Whenever Bob had tied a knot, he carefully tested it. He pulled tightly on his line on each side of the knot. When my Dad lost some strength with age, he would ask me to check his knots. I never pulled hard enough to crease the sides of my hands as he used to. All of his knots withstood my testing. I don't ever recall him losing a fishing lure or hook due to a weakly tied knot.

Drift fishing in the Wood River allowed my Mom to read or enjoy nature, while my Dad cast. Periodically, my Mom would need to maneuver the canoe to keep it away from the banks. The slow-moving current would gently push the canoe downstream at a pace well-suited to fishing, bird-watching, and reading. Since there were few other canoeists on the river, it was a peaceful and quiet time. Almost no effort was involved. Of course, on the return up river the two of them usually needed to paddle together.

"Backwater, Roxy! Did you see that swirl?"

"No."

"Over there," pointing.

"Okay."

And my Mom paddled briskly to reach the spot. Once there, she held the canoe in place with some short strokes.

"There's a big fish under there."

My Dad aimed his cast perfectly, just as he'd done so many times throughout his life. My Mom watched. They waited.

"See that. Look!"

My Dad worked his lure with precision. Boom! The big Rainbow Trout struck my Dad's lure.

"He's on!"

Over the next few minutes my Dad would battle the big Rainbow. Each catch always seemed to be just like his first. Bob looked just like a young boy learning to fish—excited and eager and happy, disappointed only if he lost his fish. And, he rarely lost a fish once he'd hooked it. He always made sure to set his hook properly. So, if he ever did lose a fish, it'd be at the beginning when it struck his lure rather than later during the battle.

"Roxy, get the net ready."

My Dad would work the fish to the side of the canoe, and then my Mom would skillfully net the exhausted fish. Roxy would face the open end of the net toward my Dad. Over the years she'd perfected the skill of netting fish. She knew the exact spot where my Dad would bring the fish up. She was careful with the net not to scare the fish off in which case they'd continue to fight. Rather, she was able to surprise them and net them quickly before they ever even saw the net coming.

"Pass me a towel."

On that occasion Roxy handed Bob an old reddish hand-towel. He would carefully unhook the fish, and then wipe his hands on the towel. If he deemed the catch a real good one, he would ask Roxy to take a picture of him with the fish. Many times Bob took pictures of Roxy holding fish. He loved and needed her dearly. In this case Bob held the prized Rainbow Trout up. She sure was patient.

Through the years my Mom had become quite a skilled photographer. On that occasion she snapped a beautiful picture of her husband, doing what he enjoyed the most. She aimed the camera. What she saw was not just my Dad clothed as described, but she saw a happy man with his prized catch. Roxy centered him in the middle of the lens—Bob's fishing-pole visible off to the left and resting at a 45-degree angle, the edge of the frequently-used net and its green nylon mesh, the reddish hand-towel resting on Bob's thigh, Bob's face peering happily around the Rainbow Trout, and in the foreground in Bob's left hand a huge Rainbow clutched by the gills and still dripping water off its spotted tail.

Behind Bob on this autumn day sat the river. The water flowed calmly in this stretch and reflected the fall colors. Some of the leaves had already fallen off the trees, as the foliage had just passed peak. Leaves drifted serenely in the water, unsure of their destinations. Below, Rainbow Trout swam knowing that they needed to feed, but also knowing that Bob Greenlaw fished in the area. His respect for fish was great, and fish seemed to have a great respect for him. That fact made his catches all the more impressive.

Figures

A young Bob with a very long catch.

Bob holding the morning's catch.

Bob holding a trophy Largemouth Bass.

The author happily netting
a Pickerel caught on a Rebel.

The author and his
father holding a limit catch.

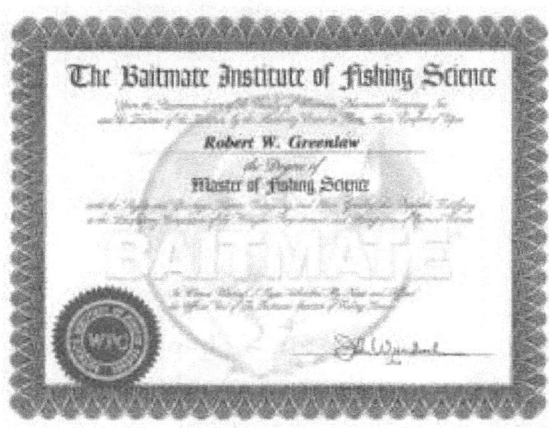

Bob's Master of Fishing Science diploma.

Roxy holding a six-pound-plus Largemouth Bass.

Bob at one of his favorite
Lighthouses in South Portland, Maine.

The author subduing *the* angry geese.

Bob with the beautiful Rainbow Trout.

Bob with a big Trout caught in the
Wood River on a "Thomas Bougout Spoon."

Roxy displaying a Smallmouth Bass.

Rob holding large White Perch.

Bob with a good-sized Largemouth Bass.

Roxy at Chapman Pond.

Bob dressed in his Ironman Canada T-shirt.

The author with a large Tautaug.

Bob with a huge Snapper.

Bob with two Alaskan Salmon.

After a long day in Alaskan waters, Bob heading back to the Cross Sound Lodge.

Bob at the dock with a barn-door Halibut.

Bob reluctantly holding his
world-record American Eel.

Bob with his world-record Shortnose Gar.

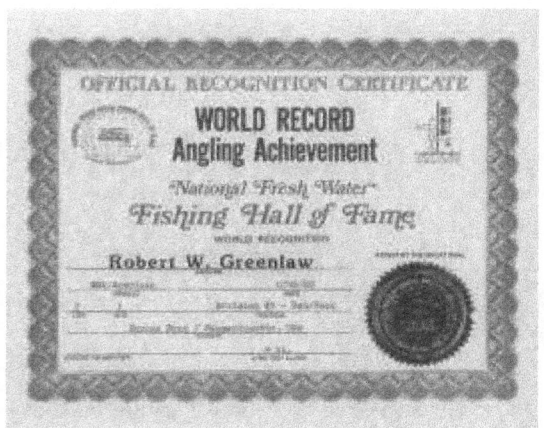

Bob's first world-record catch.

Bob's second world-record catch.

The certified lab's tests of Bob's fishing-line for his world-record Shortnose Gar catch.

Bob in Lakeland, Florida with
a 27-inch Bowfin. Notice that his
fishing license is prominently displayed.

Bob with a 20-inch Channel Catfish.

A smiling Bob among some large leaves.

A watercolor of Koi by Bob.

Bob's card.

Bob working on a piece of Scrimshaw.

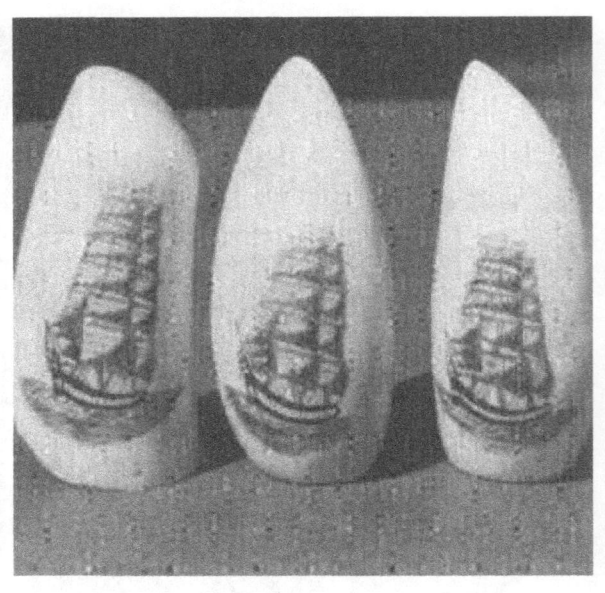

Three pieces of Bob's Scrimshaw.

The famous calendar Pickerel photograph.

On the far left in the middle,
note Bob with his calendar Pickerel.

The author's big
Pickerel which Scott scooped.

Bob and his son Ray, the author.

In Loving Memory of

Robert W. Greenlaw

September 12, 1927

August 19, 2000

Sunset and evening star,
And one clear call from me!
And may there be no moaning
of the bar
When I put out to sea.
But such a tide as moving seems
asleep,
Too full for sound and foam,
When that which drew from out
the boundless deep
Turns again home.
Twilight and evening bell,
And after that the dark!
And may there be no sadness
of farewell, When I embark;
For tho' from out our bourne
of Time and place
The flood may bear me far, I hope
to see my Pilot face to face
When I have crossed the bar.

Watson Funeral Home

Bob's Memorial Service Remembrance.

Chapter 6
Trout Fisherman Captured

Neither my Dad nor I classified as great paddlers. We paddled the canoe to reach our fishing spots; we rarely canoed for the sake of canoeing itself. I never remember a time going out in a canoe with my Dad and not bringing along fishing-gear. Through mere repetition and time spent in the boat, we became relatively skilled canoeists and could, when we needed to, move the vessel quickly and adeptly. While fishing in a pond, our only paddling challenge would be if the wind came up. We usually beat the wind by getting an early start. From time-to-time we would get caught in a strong headwind and have a long hard paddle back across open water. On such crossings resting wasn't an option because the canoe would be pushed backward in the waves. Such times were few and far between.

After a heavy rainfall fishing can be quite good. The increased river volume allows fish to feed in areas that they previously couldn't access. Storms and strong winds associated with heavy rains knock lots of insects into the water. River currents increase, too, and generally fish seem more active. Perhaps this fact is in part due to the cooling effect of the rain water. High water can be dangerous for inexperienced canoeists, but if it looked safe to us, we would fish immediately after a storm. We weren't going to pass up any good opportunities.

On the particular day in question my Dad and I were canoeing downstream heading back to our car after a day of successful fishing. The cooler preserved our catch, and we'd already eaten the lunch that Roxy had prepared. We weren't in a great rush, but the current moved us along swiftly. We didn't plan to fish again that day, unless we saw a sign from a large fish.

Traditionally, my Dad and I headed upstream first on a fishing-trip. This strategy ensured that the most vigorous paddling occurred when we felt freshest. Canoes are sleek boats, but in a strong current it can be difficult to make upstream progress. A day in the sun on the water can be draining, and we would usually be quite tired on the return paddle, even while going downstream.

At a trip's end we always faced the unloading of the canoe, a carry to the car, the lifting of the canoe onto the top of the car and the securing of it, an hour or so drive, the unloading and washing of the equipment, and then the cleaning of the fish. We usually followed that with quick baths and dinner. Thus at day's end we never wanted to have to paddle upstream for any real distance. Our energy levels were too low, and we needed to conserve our available energy for the remaining chores. Amazingly, my Dad always found the energy to clean all of the fish. My Dad kept himself in shape and always seemed to have a high-energy level. Later in life, I came to appreciate more exactly how high my Dad's energy level was. I've met very few people over the years who maintained the type of energy level that my Dad did.

When rounding corners in the rushing river, I would sometimes use a sweep stroke from the back of the boat. Sweeping hard on the right meant that I could angle the canoe gradually to the left. If done properly, we could round corners without losing any momentum. As our paddling continued, it was clear that we'd rowed upstream much farther than we'd thought. Strokes in the morning push the boat farther than strokes in the afternoon. A lot of our travel at this point meant just steering the canoe though.

The leaves on the trees appeared full and glistening with water droplets. The dense brush on the high banks of the river made some of our corners blind. We'd paddled this stretch earlier that day, and we knew that there were no stationary obstacles in the river—nothing we needed to avoid. I don't remember talking much on the paddle home other than responding to my Dad's occasional directions of "Sharp left" or "Hard right." Sometimes I let my head hang, as I dug at the water with my paddle.

I would reach forward with my wooden paddle and draw back hard on the water—my shoulders, legs, and back doing the majority of the work. By using the proper motion one's arms didn't get tired too quickly. We were used to paddling a couple of times per week, so our hands didn't blister. Once in a while, we would switch sides to balance the fatigue in our bodies. I could steer the boat better if I paddled on the right-hand side, and when a tricky section approached, we coordinated our efforts, so that I was paddling on the right.

My Dad indicated a sharp left ahead. We came flying around a blind corner, both of us paddling strongly to avoid losing any momentum. I pulled at the water with all my might; I could see that my

Dad did the same. The canoe wasn't being steered so much as powered around this corner—a significant noisy wake coming off the rear. To our utter amazement, in the center of the river stood a stunned-looking Trout fisherman.

If any group of fishermen have an elitist attitude, it's the Trout fishermen. Trout fishermen revere other Trout fishermen, and they look down upon other types of fishermen. In the one second that I had to pass judgment, based on his demeanor and his clothing, I could see that this guy fit the stereotype. He wore very expensive gear.

This Trout fisherman sported a tan fishing-vest. He stood in the middle of the river in tall green waders. Forty feet of his line flew in the air, as he was mid-cast. With an almost magnetic attraction the tip of our canoe headed directly for the space between the Trout fisherman's legs. He helplessly and hopelessly tried to move out of our way. The man flailed, shocked and immobile. His last-ditch effort to run away in waders failed miserably. The guy's line became badly tangled. My Dad glanced back at me for a brief second, a huge smile on his face, more of a funny smirk, really. I couldn't help but smile a big smile back.

Destiny had decided that this Trout fisherman would be the Greenlaws' passenger. The canoe swept up the fisherman between the legs. He straddled our fast-moving boat in the swift river. The man faced his jurors. The canoe had pronounced him guilty of believing that he was the only person on earth. His expression was not one of joy. The man showed disgust and disdain all over his face. I knew that my Dad fought valiantly to restrain his laughter; I did the same.

My Dad and I ferried the unsuspecting fellow at least one-hundred yards downstream. He couldn't escape his plight at this velocity. In fact, the question was more could he ride this bull without getting dragged underneath it. His green waders dangled over the sides of our craft, while his bottom rested on the bow. The rider tried to balance himself. His expensive fly-fishing pole waved erratically in mid-air, further tangling his line. With his other hand he clutched desperately to the rope that attached to the bull's neck, that is, our anchor line.

The man's mouth ran a series of expletives, as he scorched our ears. His tone of voice certainly wasn't friendly. At last we gained control of the canoe, and brought our unwanted passenger ashore. He continued raging about his lift. Distance- and time-wise his ride may have been one of the more notable in rodeo history; it wasn't one of the more elegant ones, though.

My Dad responded, but somehow I held my tongue. The fellow's fishing line looked akin to a bowl of spaghetti. The self-proclaimed elitist wouldn't be fishing again any time soon, plus he faced a difficult walk upstream to return to "his" spot. After dumping the guy near the river's edge, we quickly paddled around the next river bend. There our laughter overpowered us. We roared and rowed. Then we merely roared, as we could no longer row from our doubled-over positions.

My Dad spun around in his seat to face me. Our laughter increased. The fellow must have heard us. All of Rhode Island heard us. We'd tried desperately to get out of his ear-shot before our uncontrolled outburst, but I don't think that we'd succeeded. We couldn't have. My abdomen hurt. My Dad's must have, too.

"Did you see the look on that guy's face?" I roared.

My Dad laughed outrageously and in a somewhat higher-pitched voice than normal said, "I thought he was going to hit me."

"I can't believe that."

I too thought that the guy would start swinging at any moment. If his hands had been free, he probably would've. Luckily, his hands weren't as violent as his tongue.

"He was sitting right there," my Dad said pointing inches away toward the front of the canoe.

"Yeah! Boy, was he mad!"

We roared and roared. I peed my pants. We both teared up. I thought of the guy trudging upstream against the current. Surely there weren't any more trout to be had in that section of the river. His day of fishing was probably done.

The remainder of our canoe trip went smoothly and swiftly. It no longer seemed like a long boring paddle back. I never forgot the look on the Trout fisherman's face, and to this day that experience was one of the funniest incidents I've ever witnessed. I felt blessed to have shared it with my Dad. You had to be there to comprehend how hysterical the situation was.

Chapter 7
Calendar Pickerel

My Dad used to love to lie in the sun. During his generation, no warnings were ever issued about skin cancer, and sun-block didn't exist. As it became clear that the sun's rays could damage one's skin and perhaps even cause death in the case of malignant melanoma, my Dad took much-greater care when he went outdoors. In particular, he often wore a sun hat while out fishing. Sunlight that reflects off the water is very intense, though.

Bob enjoyed wearing his white tennis hat. The hat fit like a bowl, but the lid's vents and cotton fabric meant that it felt cool and made up for its appearance. The droopy sides meant that my Dad's ears didn't get burned. Beneath the brim of the hat my Dad's thick glasses rested on his nose. Polycarbonate lenses with greater refractive indexes had significantly reduced the thickness of his and my lenses compared with our older, glass-and-plastic ones. I preferred lightweight German frames, and these caught on with my Dad, too. His powerful lenses were supported by a tiny but skillfully-engineered piece of metal. With his glasses perched on his nose, Bob looked like a scientist and an erudite man. My Dad looked like he belonged in a research lab. And, he probably did.

Pickerel are known for being good fighters. These bony fish can wiggle their muscular bodies in every direction. They're capable of biting through almost anything, except wire leaders, and when running, they can pull off large quantities of line in open water. Pickerel lie still in the water waiting for their prey to swim past. Then violently and unsuspectingly they lunge, open their huge, tooth-filled mouths, and chomp on their prey. I once caught an eighteen-inch-long Pickerel only to find that it'd consumed an eight-inch-long Pickerel, so they're cannibals as well. They'll eat anything alive that they can fit into their mouths. If something moves in front of one's face, he'll strike quickly.

I never enjoyed eating Pickerel because they're so full of bones. Even Bob couldn't clean a Pickerel too well. So, I rarely kept a Pickerel. In fact, one of the few Pickerels that I remember taking home was caught on a fishing-trip with my friend Scott. Scott and I attended high school together, and were friends from both class and the cross-country team. We took some epic fishing trips during our high-school years.

My Dad never drank much beer; however, Scott and I made up for that. On the day in question Scott and I went out fishing in my Dad's canoe. Between us rested a cooler filled with food and two six-packs. As runners, we ate a lot. During those times, we enjoyed St. Pauli Girl—an expensive beer by our standards and one of the early imports. Neither one of us had been to Germany, but we'd heard about Oktober Fest. As the number of empties increased, so did the amount of fantasizing about the German St. Pauli Girl. This buxom blonde carried two fistfuls of liter beers. We admired her strength. Her low white top showed off her plentiful cleavage. Her big eyes and wide smile gave us something to dream about at night.

Scott and I had parked and anchored the canoe on the edge of the river. I cast repeatedly into some fast-moving water with my three-inch, black-and-silver Rebel. Scott enjoyed the scenery and quaffed beer. I knew there had to be a big Pickerel lurking in that water; I instinctively knew it. After five or so casts to the same spot, I almost gave up. We'd often say "Just one more cast" or "This is my last cast." Then we'd continuing casting in the same spot for a while. In this case I said the latter. Then Boom!

A huge Pickerel pounded my Rebel, and almost bit it in half. I battled the monster in the swift-moving water, while Scott opened another Girl. He kicked back and watched my struggle. I adjusted the drag. Zip, zip, zeep. This fish wanted line, and I gave it to him. When the first wanted more line, he got it. My reel was loaded with six-pound-class monofilament, and I wasn't using a wire leader. At any moment this beast could bite through the line. Valiantly, I fought on, but in the long run I suspected that I would lose. Eventually, his chomping jaws would find my thin line and his razor-sharp teeth would quickly cut through it.

The massive Pickerel broke the surface a number of times. Big splashes excited us, as did seeing parts of the fish. The fish jerked his head from side to side trying to shake the Rebel out of his big mouth.

"Did you see the size of that monster?" I shouted.

"Yeah. Wow! The tail was huge!"

"Get the net ready!"

Scott guzzled the remainder of his beer. We'd no convenient way of balancing a half-full beer in the canoe. If he'd set the green bottle down with any liquid remaining in it, the beer would've been spilled during this battle. The canoe was rocking back and forth. Scott had no qualms about draining his beer quickly.

"Ready?"

The Pickerel splashed, and splashed again. It whipped its tail violently, sending spray a long distance. I fought on, and so did the big fish. He was made of nothing, but muscle and teeth.

"Wow!"

We stared agape at the size and the energy of this fish. My fishing-pole arched dramatically. I fought hard to gain a few feet. It was a grand tug-a-war contest that I now seemed to be winning. I'd turned the tide, or had I? The fish seemed to be getting tired. I knew that I was too.

"Scott, you ready?"

"Yeah."

"I'm gonna bring this monster to you."

I tilted my pole toward the front end of the boat, and the Pickerel was forced in Scott's direction.

"Net him. Net him. Net him!" I yelled, while panicking.

Scott held only a tiny hand net. We didn't have the large aluminum net that my Dad and I always used. The fish dove. As soon as the fish had spotted Scott and the net, he found a burst of energy. And, out of fear for his life, he made a dash for the bottom of the river.

"Sorry."

"Dammit!"

The Pickerel had summoned all of its remaining strength in one final effort to avoid Scott. Fortunately, the beast was still hooked. I worked diligently again to raise the monster from the bottom. I leaned back and moved the pole with my motion. Then I quickly bent forward and reeled in the small amount of real estate that I'd gained. My lower back tired. I repeated the process a couple of more times. I was gaining. The momentum once again seemed to have turned in my favor.

"Don't miss him this time."

"Okay, man."

I successfully brought the fish Scott's way a second time. Scott held himself away from the edge of the canoe so that the fish wouldn't see him and get spooked again.

"Net him! Net …"

I watched helplessly as Scott leaned way outside the normal limits of the canoe. "Shit, we're going over," I thought. The fish appeared too big to fit into the net's opening. I felt frustrated that I'd forgotten the big net. This case would be closed, if I'd only remember the big net. My Dad never forgot anything. No sense on punishing myself further for the rookie mistake. We had to make do with the tools that we had.

"Net him!"

"He won't fit."

"Scoop him!"

Scott swiped back and forth. The fish dodged the net. I struggled to keep the fish at surface level. Finally, Scott's outreached arm positioned the net beneath the monster. With a forceful upward sweeping motion, Scott lifted the beast into the boat. Thud! The Pickerel didn't like being on the floor of the canoe. He flapped loudly beating the canoe like a drum. The fish hadn't really ever even entered the net. Scott had used the net like a broom to sweep the beast into the boat.

"Subdue him. He'll jump out. Quickly!"

Eventually, Scott controlled the situation, while employing an empty St. Pauli Girl. He smashed the beast with her breasts.

"Nice catch."

"Thanks."

"Amazing!"

"I'm keeping this one to show my Dad! I can't believe we landed him."

The Pickerel weighed in one ounce shy of the world record for six-pound-class line. Its large teeth poked out in every direction and were impressive—plentiful, sharp, and dangerous. The Rebel had been embedded in the fish's mouth in such a way that he'd been unable to sever my line. Had those teeth touched the line at all, it would've been cut instantly. If I hadn't kept high tension on the line at all times, the biting motions of the fish would've broken the line. I felt lucky. I'd been using the techniques that made Dad had taught me.

The two us celebrated the enormous and improbable catch with a St. Pauli Girl. We relaxed for a while, admired the Girl on the bottles, and then moved downstream, heading back toward the car. The beers had all disappeared, and in the hot sun we felt buzzed—happy, content, and relaxed. We used to say, "This is the life." As we paddled gently downstream, I saw a big fish swirl. I was thinking that *it* was the world-record fish. Maybe it was even bigger than the monster that we'd already caught.

"Weigh anchor man; did you see that?" I exclaimed excitedly.

Scott followed my instructions, and he tossed the anchor overboard. We watched in disbelief. Both of us had completely forgotten that Scott had untied the anchor in order to use the anchor line as a chain stringer for the monster Pickerel. Since the Pickerel didn't fit in the cooler, we'd preserved it in the water.

"Backwater, backwater!" I shouted, as my amazement subsided, and I could speak again.

"Shit!"

"Backwater."

The two of us did an immediate U-turn and headed upstream. Our problem was that we'd already traveled on the order of 100 yards, or was it 200? We needed to find that anchor. I wasn't returning home sans anchor. I felt responsible for my Dad's fishing-gear, and I certainly wasn't going to lose his favorite anchor. I shook my head in disbelief at the situation in which we now found ourselves. The Girls clearly had impaired our judgment.

My brother Rob used my Dad's fishing-gear on occasion, and I know that Rob felt the same way about my Dad's things as I did. Neither one of us would ever damage or lose an item; we took great care of and responsibility for our Dad's equipment. The one time that I remember something going wrong, I heard my brother discussing a broken paddle with my Dad. The paddle was smashed to smithereens.

Rob's story went along the lines that a large Northern Water Snake had attacked him, and that he'd pounded the life-threatening snake to death using the paddle—his only available weapon to defend against the fast-approaching attacker. It appeared that my Dad didn't buy into this tale, until Rob produced the headless creature from the trunk of his car. In the event that my Dad might have doubted the far-reaching story, Rob had brought the proof home. My Dad simply stared at the serpent in disbelief, while shaking his head from side-to-side.

Scott and I spent about 30 minutes locating the place where he'd tossed the anchor overboard. On scanning the shore a dozen or so times, we thought that we recalled where I'd seen the large swirl, which had initially prompted me to ask Scott to weigh anchor. I held the canoe in place with some steady strokes. Was this spot the right one?

"Do you mind going in?"

No response came, but Scott stripped down. The water felt cold to him, but he eased in without capsizing us. The depth of the water measured about five feet, so Scott could stand on his toes; however, the current pushed him gently along. His feet stirred up the bottom, too, obstructing our vision. We had no goggles, so he couldn't see much when he dove. I felt for sure that we'd come up empty handed. Our search persisted, and Scott seemed to be sobering up from being in the cold water so long. After another 20 minutes of discussion and recovery efforts, Scott felt the anchor with his toe.

"I've got it, Ray!"

Scott dove and emerged with the anchor, which he handed to me.

"Whew. Thanks," I said while taking hold of the anchor.

I'd maintained the boat's position throughout Operation Anchor Recovery. Scott climbed back into the canoe, while I hunkered down to lower our center-of-gravity. In jest Scott threatened to capsize us, but in the long run he didn't. As time had quickly passed, we went straight home. My Dad was extremely impressed by the size of the trophy

Pickerel. Scott snapped a Polaroid. I never told my Dad the story about the anchor.

There was an unspoken friendly fishing competition between my Dad and me. We always liked to one-up the other person in fishing terms. So, although my Dad didn't normally fish for Pickerel, my monster catch had inspired him. On the particular day in question, Bob and Roxy embarked alone in the canoe.

Bob wore his sun hat and a light-colored, short-sleeved, golf shirt. Undoubtedly, Roxy and he had the large net on board. That day Bob hooked into a monster Pickerel. The battle must've been epic—violent splashes, flaps, and swirls. Commands flew, "Roxy, move the canoe forward," "Roxy, backwater," "Get the net ready," and "Net him, Roxy." My parents won that victory, and I'm sure in a much-more, elegant fashion than the battle that Scott and I'd waged and won.

Roxy snapped a professional-photographer's-quality image of my Dad, while he held up his near world-record Pickerel. Bob positioned the fish at chest level with one hand beneath the gills and the other near the tail; the Pickerel stretched far past Bob's shoulders on both sides, and Bob's hands pointed outward. My Dad's white sun-hat nicely blended with the green colors of the spotted Pickerel. Bob looked like a proud old fisherman—the old fisherman on the sea. I envisioned my mother on the other side of the camera, patient, kind, caring, and loving, happy to take Bob's picture on this important occasion, creating a memory for their children and grandchildren.

At that time Bob was getting up there in years. I seriously doubted that anyone his age had ever hauled in a Pickerel as big, and for that matter Bob's Pickerel may have been the second- or third-largest ever caught—the world-record fish, my fish, and Bob's fish or the world-record fish, Bob's fish, and my fish—depending on whom you spoke to.

Each year Rhode Islanders put out a seniors' calendar which depicts senior citizens participating in various activities. Roxy's picture of my Dad holding the huge Pickerel garnered the month of August 2000, but more impressively, it also was the cover photo for the calendar for the entire year. The image greatly deserved its positioning, and my Dad had once again immortalized himself through his fishing exploits.

Chapter 8
Alaskan Halibut

All serious anglers dream of fishing in Alaska. Many world-record fish have come from those deep and cold waters. The idyllic images of Alaska—beautiful mountain scenery, bald eagles soaring overhead, and whales blowing mist high into the air—meant that it was just a matter of time before my Dad and I ventured to the last frontier with fishing in mind. I'm so glad that we once shared a trip to Cross Island Sound, Alaska.

My Dad and I were both accustomed to traveling. He traveled frequently on business to attend conferences and to visit earthquake-sites. We once took a field trip together with a group of seismologists from Cal Tech. Most of the country's major fault lines are located on the West Coast. Bob enjoyed California. Although I was one of only a few students from my high-school class of 750 who was accepted by Brown University, my Dad encouraged me to venture out to Pomona College in Southern California. I'm so glad that I followed his advice. That move broadened my perspective at an important time in my life. And, Pomona College has been the number one ranked school of any university in the United States many times.

My Dad and I'd flown across the country together several times, but this time we met in Anchorage. After touring the capital city of Alaska and taking the "obligatory" tourist photographs, my Dad and I embarked on a one-week fishing trip. We boarded a tiny bi-plane, and we flew to a private remote Alaskan island, which consisted mainly of a couple of fishing-lodges. The spectacular flight carried us over majestic forest and many Bull Moose. The plane was so small that we each had window seats. Rivers flowed in every conceivable direction, and we imagined world-class Salmon swimming below us. We planned to eat a great deal of fresh seafood on this trip. My favorite food is Alaskan King Crab Legs, and my Dad truly enjoyed Salmon and Halibut. Of course, what really got our blood flowing was the thought of landing a giant Alaskan fish.

My Dad's early fishing-career began in fresh water. Later, when he'd acquired a motor boat, he fished primarily in salt water. Once his kids were grown, and the boat became a bit too-much work, he reverted primarily to fresh water. Bob always fished both fresh and salt water, though. In salt water his favorite fish to catch were Blue Fish, Cod, Flounder, Haddock, Halibut, Mackerel, Perch, Pollock, Red Snapper, Salmon, Striped Bass, and Tautaug, among others. On this trip we hoped to land some gigantic Halibut and some huge Salmon. We both dreamed of reeling in absolutely enormous fish. Such dreams keep fishermen going.

I loved to eat Flounder, especially the way my Mom prepared it. When my good friend Pete and I would go out to dinner, if the fish tasted extraordinarily good, Pete would say, "Just like Roxy's." So, whenever we caught Flounder and my Mom cooked it fresh, that was a true joy. I've paid exorbitant prices for a serving of Flounder at various top-notch, seafood restaurants, but never has anyone's Flounder approached my Mom's cooking in taste. The simplicity of her New England cooking satisfied my palate wonderfully.

Flounder aren't the most attractive fish to look at. In fact, God may have made a mistake. Flounder are also known as Flatfish; they're indeed flat. Flounder are so flat that both eyes are on the same side of their "head." In reality they don't have a head in the traditional sense, but rather a triangle.

Their eyes sit side-by-side near the tip of their triangle. Halibut are closely related to Flounder. The main difference is that Halibut are huge, like Flounders on steroids. Neither of these types of fish have large brains. One could easily say that Halibut are the Brontosaurus of fish. Make no mistake about their will-power to live though. They'll put up an amazing fight from great depths.

Halibut, like Flounder, are inherently ugly—one side is gray and smeared with spots, while the other is completely white, almost see-through. Halibut are proportionally flat, but since they grow so huge, they can be rather thick. Halibut is an expensive game-fish, and most people agree that it's delicious eating. My Dad and I figured that with all of the fillets which we planned to return home with we would more than pay for our trip. In fact, giving away packets of the Halibut to our family and friends would give us enough pleasure that the price of the trip really wasn't that important to us.

Each morning our group, the only group at the lodge, would get a Rooster's start. The lodge staff fed us an American breakfast. Thank God, I had just completed the Western States 100-Mile Endurance Run a few days earlier. I felt emaciated, so I could take advantage of the food. My Dad's appetite couldn't match mine, although he ate a great deal for a thin man.

As an endurance athlete, that is, an ultra-marathon runner, long-distance hiker, and an Ironman triathlete, I would acquire finishers T-shirts from my races. I gave many of these T-shirts to my Dad, as we actually wore the same size. He sported them proudly. With phrases such as "expect excellence," "world's toughest triathlon," and "100-mile endurance run" plastered on his chest, he got lots of stares. Many conversations with strangers and Bob began when they asked him if he was an Ironman or endurance athlete. My Mom told me that my Dad enjoyed such conversations immensely, and that he was extremely proud of me. I feel good about that.

After devouring way too many calories, we would board our 38-foot fishing charter. My Dad and I fished with a group of eight. Several of the guys were hard-core fishermen, and we exchanged many stories with them—usually about our biggest catches or about the biggest fish that we'd lost. Of course, the ones that we lost were always far, far larger in size than the ones that we actually caught. Like all fishermen, each of us was prone to a bit of exaggeration. While out on the boat, its owner's yellow Labrador retriever alerted us to approaching fish, including whales. The dog would race back-and-forth along the boat's deck barking wildly. The hair standing up on his back, and his tail moving around like a bouncy spring. We enjoyed looking at both Humpbacks and Orcas up close. My Dad paid careful attention to the form of the Humpbacks, and they influenced his Scrimshaw.

Alaska is a special place. My Dad and I felt blessed to be there fishing together. The sheer size of Alaska and the size of the animals there is breath taking. With Bald Eagles soaring overhead and Sea Lions swimming nearby, it'd be hard to image a more-beautiful scene in nature. The sounds of the waves hitting the boat, and the sounds of the blow holes on the whales taking a breath were sounds that we never got tired of hearing. The fresh smell of the salt water and of fish filled our noses. Occasionally, we'd feel mist on our faces too. All of our senses were fully engaged in the Alaskan fishing experience.

After a full day's worth of fishing, we would return to the dock. It felt good to get back into sheltered and calm waters, especially after having expended so much energy hauling in our catch. The boat's gigantic coolers bulged with large Halibut and Salmon. The two of us knew that we would each be going home with 150 pounds of fillets. I planned to give away a lot of my fish to friends; my Dad planned to eat the bulk of his catch with Roxy, but there'd still be some left over to distribute among family and friends.

When fishing for Halibut, we would bait our large hooks with a chunk of Salmon and lower the line to the bottom, using a heavy weight. Halibut feed along the bottom in 300-feet-deep water. Three hundred feet is a long distance to pull in a 100-pound fish. In fact, reeling in 300 feet of line on a large reel is a small workout in and of itself. When a muscular fish is fighting against you, 300 feet is a long, long way. We fished with poles called Ugly Sticks. These heavy-weight poles bent insignificantly, unless a fish weighed over 50 pounds. Thus if we saw a pole arching, we knew that we had connected with a monster.

Bob was something to watch. Around his slender waist he had attached a leather fish-pole holder. This belt allowed him to place the butt end of his fishing-pole directly below waist level. For thin guys like us, while pulling in a 100-pounder, it would've been impossible to hold the fishing-pole directly against one's stomach. As the big fish worked Bob over, we would say things like "You've got a barn door" or "He doesn't want anything but line" or "Come on, Bob; you got 'im on the run." If Bob looked particularly tired, we offered more encouragement: "Just a bit more" or "Hang in there, you're making great progress." Most of the time we were all laughing and smiling. We did a lot of back slapping, "You're the man" or "You showed him."

By the time Bob raised a 100-pounder to the surface, he was exhausted but overjoyed. He felt relieved and happy to have pulled up such a giant. The Halibut were so big and dangerous that we actually needed to shoot them before bringing them on board. With one flick of a tail, a giant Halibut could break a human's leg. Even though the fish were exhausted, we couldn't take any chances. The yellow Lab ran around the boat barking like crazy when a catch neared the surface or was pulled on board. Everyone snapped pictures. A great deal of excitement filled the air.

Now imagine the contrast between our freshwater-fishing trips in the New England and this trip in Alaska. Start with the boat size. We were used to fishing in a canoe in calm waters. Here we were on a small yacht fishing in rough seas. We were really exposed to the forces of nature. Rather than pulling in a Largemouth Bass or a Perch that weighed a couple of pounds, we were pulling in fish that were regularly more than half of our own body weight. Rather than seeing Blue Jays and Sparrows, we were watching soaring Bald Eagles and Osprey. Rather than a Muskrat we were looking at Sea Lions. Instead of lifting a fish directly into the canoe, we were blasting its brains out with a shotgun before bringing it on board. Rather than a Sewing Needle fluttering down and landing peacefully on the side of our canoe, we had an overly excited golden running up-and-down barking wildly. Our situation was completely foreign to what we were accustomed to, but we fully embraced it and thoroughly enjoyed each moment. This experience was the one that we'd been dreaming about for many years.

For the most part we lucked out with the weather on our Alaskan trip. We could see the Alaska Range Mountains almost every day. These glaciated peaks excited me, as I knew that one day I would return with my Dad's spirit to climb Mount McKinley. (In fact, I did go back to summit Denali on May 26, 2009 which was a few years after I wrote the first edition of this book.) When we approached any rock outcroppings along the shore, we saw Seals basking in the sun. With Bald Eagles hovering over us and towering trees lining the shore, we fished in paradise. I wished that all young men and women had a chance to share an experience like this one with their fathers and mothers.

Although most fishermen drink lots of alcohol, my Dad consumed very little. During dinner the other guys would toss back a few hard drinks, and I would usually drink a beer to two. But my Dad didn't drink. Bob was reserved. He would wake up early each morning and go for a walk on the piers. The network of wooden piers gave him a one-mile course, which he covered several times each morning. I remember one morning when he woke me up to tell me that he'd slipped badly. He didn't get hurt, but the slip had jostled him and shaken him up. My Dad didn't want to miss any of his regular morning walks, even while on holiday on a tiny island. My father showed great discipline and dedication to remaining healthy. Bob was a creature of habit.

During our week of fishing, my Dad and I enjoyed each other's company. Since I'd lived on the West Coast and later in northern New England, my Dad and I didn't see each other as often as we wanted to. It felt good to spend some quality time together. I'm so happy that we did. The fishing was outstanding, and the memories created treasures. We never really expressed our feelings directly to each other, but we didn't need to. Our father-son relationship bonded us together in a special way.

The rough seas of the Alaskan coast had taken a toll on us, though, so when our week ended we were ready to head home to our families. We'd caught huge Halibut, Salmon, Cod, Snapper, Skates, and several other species of fish. Our catch had been filleted and vacuum-packed. I'd eaten my share of Alaskan King Crab Legs, and my Dad had eaten his share of Salmon and Halibut. Our biplane loaded up, we were ready to fly back to Anchorage. The dream fishing trip was coming to an end.

Luckily for me, I sat in the co-pilot's seat in the cockpit during our return flight. This seat gave me tremendous viewing opportunities, a real bird's-eye view. The take-off felt dicey. The plane cargo's maxed out its limit. Carrying the heavy fishermen, the tackle, and our enormous catch, the plane had difficultly clearing the tall Alaskan forest. I watched speechless, as we brushed tree-tops rising from another small island. To be honest with you, I was very content at that moment. And, if one has to die in such a situation, well, at that moment I could've accepting going down in that plane with my Dad. At last, we seemed airborne above the forest and over the water. A Humpback Whale put on a spectacular show for us with a full breach. His splash went out a good 150 feet in all directions. I'd never seen a full breach before, but I did see one in the Cook Islands many years later. The whale appeared to hang in the air for a full second before gravity intervened. My Dad's was memorized by the whale's show.

At the baggage check-in in Anchorage, coolers, boxes of vacuum-packed fish, suitcases, and assorted fishing-gear covered the floor. We checked in for our flight destinations: Me to New Hampshire and my Dad to Rhode Island. My Dad and I firmly embraced, and then gave each other a strong hand-shake, which was characteristic of my Dad. There may have been a tear in his eye. I had trouble keeping my eyes dry. I thank him for a wonderful time, and he thanked me giving me one final pat on the back. We headed to our separate flight gates. It was the trip of a lifetime to be shared with my father, the man who gave me unconditional love.

Epilogue

My father died unexpectedly on August 21, 2000. It was the same month that his giant Pickerel had graced the cover of the seniors' calendar. I got the call from my mother on a Saturday morning while I was working at my office in Savannah, Georgia.

She said in a very serious tone and with great sadness in her voice, "Ray, I have something to tell you."

And, I replied, "Go ahead, Mom."

To which she said, "Raymond, your father died this morning."

I remember falling to my knees in tears, "Love you, Mom. I'm so sorry. I'll talk to you later." That was all I could manage at that desperate moment.

I knew that my mother was far stronger than I. I couldn't possibly console her at that time. I could barely even speak. I felt a horrible sickness sweep over me. It felt as though my heart had burst open into a million tiny pieces. A giant empty hole filled my stomach. After hanging up the phone, I went out for a 10-mile run. I cried the entire way. Those who I ran by asked if I was okay, as they could clearly see the distressed state that I was in. I was a broken man. I lied to them. Eventually, my Mom and I were able to talk more when I could regain my speech, and I was soon able to talk to my siblings. The next day I traveled to Rhode Island to be with my family.

At my Dad's memorial service, I made the following comments:

Thanks, Rob.

Mom, Gina, Roberta, Rob, family members, and dear friends, we are here today to celebrate and remember the life of Robert Wilson Greenlaw (I was sobbing but I carried on):

Beloved husband, beloved father (I took a long pause and wiped away my tears), and beloved friend. (I could see many family members and friends crying, as my tears flowed freely. I knew that I was visibly shaking. But, I wanted to deliver the remarks that I'd prepared in full. I just needed to take a deep breath when I was gasping for air.)

I would like to do this by saying a few words about my Dad, by providing a list of the things that he enjoyed and knew best, by telling a fishing-tale, and by reading a poem.

Once I am finished, I would like to invite others to speak either by stepping up to the podium or talking from their seats, however they are most comfortable. Following the service, everyone is invited to my Mom's house at 82 Indian Road in Riverside for coffee and pastry.

My Dad was a renaissance man. In a day of specialization my Dad was knowledgeable about many different things, and he enjoyed learning. Dad was a doer. He enjoyed teaching and helping others. Whenever we came together, I asked him questions, for advice, and for help in performing some task. He *always* lent knowledge, experience, and a helping hand. Dad enjoyed assisting others.

As I go through a list of things my Dad enjoyed and did, please reflect with me on the happy times that you shared with him, and on the footprints that he has left on your heart and life.

Among other things, my Dad was a loving husband, father (more tears fell), grandfather, mentor, author, antiques-dealer, artist (both a Scrimshaw artist and a painter), Vice President of Allendale Mutual Insurance Company, soldier, electrician, toastmaster, mineral collector, sportsman [target shooter, boater, canoeist, fisherman—he loved Rhode Island and the Cape, tennis-player, walker—he loved to walk with my Mom], teacher, traveler, handyman, seismologist, mathematician, nuclear-power expert, student—he loved learning, world-record holder, fire-protection engineer, radio operator, and photographer—he loved to take pictures of Mom (I teared up again), and his children and their families; he displayed his pictures, and they enriched his life and ours. The photos will provide great memories and comfort to us.

My Dad loved to fish.

"Hey, did you see that swirl?"

"Roxy, start the motor!"

"It was a great big thing!"

"Rob, get your line in the water!"

"Ray, quick; cast over there!"

These phrases he would shout with exuberance and joy. His excitement and zest for fishing were contagious. Dad knew every pond in Rhode Island, their contour lines, how to access them, the type of bait or lure to use, what pound test line to use, what was biting, and so on. He loved the Cape and New England. We fished in Alaska, which gave him great happiness (and, I was able to smile). We often fished from our canoe. In our canoe my Mom paddled my Dad all over New England.

One time my Dad and I were fishing in the Wood River in Rhode Island. We were paddling downstream in a fast current around a tight turn. When we came around the corner, there was a stunned Trout fisherman standing in the middle of the river with about 40 feet of line out. The canoe straddled him, and he ended up legs split, sitting on the canoe in front of Dad's face, and being carried downstream against his will. When we dropped him off with tangled line, he had a few things to say. Dad uttered something about me not knowing how to steer. We went around the next bend of the river, and laughed so hard that we peed our pants.

There are many other stories like this as well. I will write them down. I have lots of wonderful memories (and, I knew that someday I would write this book).

My father was my friend, my mentor, and my cheerleader. My father traveled to see me; he was at my graduations and my races. My father inspired me in life; he was my hero. I wrote this poem in his loving memory. (I took another pause and a deep breath before reading on.)

Remembering Dad

A ripple in a pond on a clear summer day.
You often talked about The Big One that got away.

A brisk walk on a path at four mph.
You loved to visit us, from Georgia to NH.

I'll see you in nature, in the mountains and streams.
You will be there in the glowing sunbeams.

Memories of a lifetime that make me feel glad.
That I was fortunate to call a man like you Dad.

You are here with me; you are here in me.
I will think of you in whatever I do.

I will remember you, Dad. I love you dearly.
I will remember and love you, Dad! Most sincerely.

As I finished reading my poem, I felt a sense of relief and my shaking subsided a bit. I'd cried so much and so forcefully that my eyes were drying out. And, I was able to comprehend that my Dad and I had a good relationship. That my Dad had lived his life to the best of *his* ability. That he'd done the best that *he* could do for his family. He had supported me in the best way that *he* knew how. At that moment coming to this realization gave me a chance to move forward inch by inch. I knew that the healing process of losing my Dad, my greatest champion, would never end.

Exactly five years have passed since my Dad died (which is when I wrote the first edition of this book). I've missed him dearly each and every day. He has been with me in my travels both in the high mountains of the world and below the ocean's surface. Every day I think of him. The gap in my life caused by his death has been immeasurably huge. A big part of me departed, and I was forced to grow in new ways.

For five years I've been working up the courage to face my Dad's death, and only now have I summoned the strength to write this book, which at his memorial service I publicly promised that I would write. I wrote the table of contents for the book one month after my Dad died, but each time I tried to write the book, I couldn't carry on, until now.

Another 11 years has passed since I wrote the first edition of this book. Now again, I have revisited the book and produced a second edition. The feelings of loss persist and the emptiness left in my heart from losing my Dad is still there. The healing process continues. As relationships between fathers and sons throughout the world change, I feel that it's more important than ever to share the relationship that my Dad and I had with others. We spent a lot of time together, and that time was very important to both of our lives. Parents should always make time for their children, and children should always make time for their parents. My family taught me that lesson. And, after losing my Mom shortly after returning from Denali in 2009, the fact that we'd spent as much time together as possible is the only thing that gives me the strength to go on with my life. Miss you so much, Mom!

This book is my gift to you, Dad, to you, Mom, to my siblings, and to their families. Thanks, Dad and thanks, Mom, for loving me so completely and unconditionally. I'm absolutely blessed to have had you both for parents. You're the best parents that I could ever dream of. We'll always be together. Your loving son, Raymond.

About the Author

Raymond "Wall" Greenlaw was born in Providence, Rhode Island in 1961 to Roxy and Bob. He has always enjoyed nature, big trees, mountains, and the sea. His passion is traveling, and he now resides in Northern Thailand where he has spent a great deal of time over the past 15 years.

Other Books by Raymond Greenlaw

PALMARÈS (also available in electronic form).

The Thai Wife Story JOY (also available in electronic form), Book 1 of *The Thai Wife Series of Novels*.

The Thai Wife Story STAR (also available in electronic form), Book 2 of *The Thai Wife Series of Novels*.

Raymond's Checklist for Traveling in the USA (also available in electronic form), Book 1 of *Raymond's Checklist Series*.

Raymond's Checklist for Traveling in Thailand (also available in electronic form), Book 2 of *Raymond's Checklist Series*.

Raymond's Checklist for Traveling the World (also available in electronic form), Book 3 of *Raymond's Checklist Series*.

Raymond's Checklist for His Personal Bucket List (also available in electronic form), Book 4 of *Raymond's Checklist Series*.

Raymond's Checklist for Gear for a Long Hike (also available in electronic form), Book 5 of *Raymond's Checklist Series.*

Raymond's Checklist Cycling Gear (also available in electronic form), Book 6 of *Raymond's Checklist Series.*

The Hazards of Cycling in Thailand: Guidelines for Tourists (also available in electronic form).

Trapped in Thailand's Cave (also available in electronic form).

The Pacific Crest Trail: Its Fastest Hike, second edition (also available in electronic form).

Bob: My Dad, the Fisherman: A Father and Son's Relationship (also available in electronic form).

(With Saowaluk Rattanaudomsawat) *Essential Conversational Thai: Learn to Speak Thai Quickly, while Traveling in Thailand.*

You'll Never Walk Alone: Love Poems for My Sweetheart (also available in electronic form).

Poems of Raymond Greenlaw, 1986–2005 (also available in electronic form).

The Fastest Hike across Thailand (expected 2022).

www.ingramcontent.com/pod-product-compliance
Lightning Source LLC
LaVergne TN
LVHW041254080426
835510LV00009B/736